Let's Write

Let's Write offers a wealth of suggestions for approaches to developing primary school pupils' writing skills that will capture the children's interest, while enabling them to improve their ability to express themselves in writing. It aims to meet the requirements of the new national curriculum for English at KS2 in a way that will develop the children's standard of writing by presenting activities that they will find enjoyable and stimulating.

Throughout the book, the emphasis is on providing activities that will engage the pupils in a discussion of how texts are structured, before producing their own writing. John Foster suggests a range of imaginative tasks that both literacy specialists and non-specialists will find useful in developing children's ability to write coherently and correctly.

Let's Write includes:

- a clear explanation of the writing process with activities designed to improve pupils' drafting skills;
- examples of the different types of writing for pupils to analyse, which they can use as models for their own writing;
- a range of imaginative ideas for writing tasks, together with suggestions of curriculum opportunities for practising particular forms;
- writing challenges which can be used to stretch more able writers and thus to introduce differentiation by task, as well as by outcome;
- writing tips, for example on sentence structure and paragraph structure, appropriate to the different types of writing;
- activities involving pupils in the assessment of their writing;
- a section on writing correctly, focusing on grammar, spelling and punctuation;
- a section containing games and activities designed to extend pupils' vocabulary.

Let's Write provides a lively collection of resources that will be welcomed by teachers and that will help to develop children's writing.

John Foster taught English for twenty years before becoming a full-time writer. He has written over 100 books for classroom use and is a highly regarded children's poet, anthologist and poetry performer.

Let's Write
Activities to develop writing skills for 7–11 year olds

John Foster

Routledge
Taylor & Francis Group

LONDON AND NEW YORK

First published 2014
by Routledge
2 Park Square, Milton Park, Abingdon, Oxon OX14 4RN

and by Routledge
711 Third Avenue, New York, NY 10017

Routledge is an imprint of the Taylor & Francis Group, an informa business

British Library Cataloguing in Publication Data
A catalogue record for this book is available from the British Library

Library of Congress Cataloging in Publication Data
A catalog record for this book has been requested

ISBN: 978-0-415-72850-8 (pbk)
ISBN: 978-1-315-81849-8 (ebk)

Typeset in Helvetica
by Saxon Graphics Ltd, Derby

MIX
Paper from responsible sources
FSC® C013604

Printed and bound by CPI Group (UK) Ltd, Croydon, CR0 4YY

Contents

1 Introduction

Let's Write provides teachers of literacy with activities that are both stimulating and easy to use on all the different types of writing that pupils aged 7 to 11 are expected to do. For use in any primary classroom, this book will help develop pupils' understanding of the features of particular types of writing and improve the quality of their writing.

The four main sections each focus on a particular type of writing – personal writing, persuasive writing, information writing and creative writing. Within each section there are separate chapters on different writing genres:

- Personal writing: autobiography, diaries, journals, letters, messages and recounts.
- Persuasive writing: advertisements, arguments, blurbs, letters expressing an opinion and reviews.
- Information writing: biographies, descriptions, directions, explanations, glossaries, instructions, invitations, newspaper reports, recipes, reports (non-chronological) and summaries.
- Creative writing: stories, play-scripts, poems, jokes, traditional tales and tongue-twisters.

It is envisaged that teachers will focus on a particular form as appropriate within their schemes of work. For example, they might focus on explanations when doing a science or geography topic, and use the chapter on recounts following a class visit. The chapter on blurbs can be used when focusing on children's reading for pleasure, and that on reports when reporting a scientific experiment or writing a historical report, such as a report of how people lived in Elizabethan times. The majority of the suggestions for activities are aimed at years 5 and 6, although many of them can be adapted to make them suitable for years 3 and 4.

Each chapter offers sufficient ideas for one or more lessons on a particular form of writing and there are activity sheets, which can be either photocopied or put on the whiteboard. The activity sheets vary. Some offer models to be analysed, while others are designed to help pupils to plan and draft their writing. The aim is to enable children to identify the overall structure and shape of different texts and how they are organised and sequenced for the reader, so that they will write with coherence. The emphasis is on helping pupils to understand the features of particular forms by providing models for them to analyse and to give them practice at using the different forms.

Throughout the book there are a series of writing tips, such as how to write an opening sentence that will grab the reader's attention, how to use alliteration and the use of powerful adjectives. There are also writing challenges for more able writers, and checklists to involve pupils in assessment of their writing. In addition, where appropriate, there are suggestions of curriculum opportunities for pupils to practise a particular form of writing.

There is an introductory section explaining the writing process, which pupils need to be aware of whenever they do an extended piece of writing. It is important that you explain the distinction between redrafting and proofreading and keep constantly reminding them what redrafting involves – thinking about the language, structure and content of their writing – and that this is different from proofreading, which involves checking the accuracy of the spelling and ensuring that there are no grammatical mistakes and that the punctuation is correct.

Within the final section 'Writing correctly' there are chapters on grammar, spelling and punctuation designed to be used as appropriate with individuals or groups to help them write correctly. These chapters can also be used to prepare pupils for the level 3–5 and the level 6 grammar, spelling and punctuation tests. They provide information and activities on:

- how to recognise, write and punctuate simple, compound and complex sentences;
- the parts of speech, including the difference between proper, common and abstract nouns, and examples of collective nouns;
- the various forms of verbs, such as the infinitive, tenses and active and passive voices;
- adjectives and how to form and use comparatives and superlatives;
- the different types of adverb – manner, time, frequency and place;
- personal, relative and possessive pronouns;
- how to use prepositions;
- what standard English is and common errors that occur due to dialect differences, such as the use of double negatives, 'them' instead of 'those' and 'should of' instead of 'should have';
- simple spelling rules and ways of remembering difficult words;
- how words are formed by adding prefixes and suffixes;
- how to use full stops and capital letters, commas, semi-colons, colons, question marks and exclamation marks;
- the difference between direct and indirect speech and how to punctuate speech;
- how contractions are made and the use of the apostrophe in contractions and to show possession.

The chapter 'Vocabulary building' includes games such as 'What's the word?', activities involving finding synonyms and antonyms and alternatives to tired words.

The final chapter 'Setting targets' involves pupils in self-assessment of the development of their writing skills.

2   The writing process

It is important that you make children aware that whatever type of writing they are being asked to produce, the writing process is the same. Explain that it has a number of stages and write the stages on the board, as you explain them.

Stage 1: collecting ideas

Explain that this may involve doing research and making notes. It may involve brainstorming a topic or making a list of arguments.

This stage may also involve making a plan. It will depend on the purpose and type of writing as to whether the plan is detailed or merely an outline. It is important to stress that if a plan is made, you need to be flexible. Often, particularly in story-writing, significant ideas come to you as you write. So you need to be prepared to change your plan while you are drafting.

Stage 2: selecting ideas and writing the first draft

Explain that if you have been researching a topic or brainstorming ideas, you do not have to include everything that you thought of; rather, it is important to be selective.

This stage is often referred to as a 'rough draft'. The term 'rough' suggests that the writer need not care too much about the draft and can approach it casually. Calling it a 'rough draft' creates the wrong impression. It is far better to refer to it as a first draft.

Stage 3: redrafting

A piece of writing may go through several drafts and children need to understand that the changes they make when redrafting are improvements rather than corrections. If they decide to change a word, for example, it is not because the initial word is 'wrong', but because the word that they have chosen instead is either more suitable and more accurate, is more powerful and effective, or has particular connotations.

Explain that redrafting involves thinking about the content, the organisation and structure of the piece and the language that is used.

Stage 4: proofreading

Discuss how this stage involves checking the grammar, punctuation and spelling.

Stage 5: publishing

Explain that this means producing the final version either by printing out a copy from the word processor or writing out a 'fair copy' by hand.

Part One

Personal writing

3   Autobiographies

An autobiography is an account of a person's life which is written by that person.

Explain that an autobiography is a type of personal writing in which you write about yourself and your life. The purpose of an autobiography is to tell your reader about the interesting things that have happened in your life and to describe your thoughts and feelings about your experiences.

Discuss how the audience for your autobiography can be not only your family and friends but also other people, such as children of your age in an overseas school with which your school is linked.

Collecting ideas

Ask individual students to collect ideas for their autobiographies by noting down a list of interesting things that have happened to them in their lives. Prompt them to think about things such as:

- where they have lived;
- things they have achieved;
- places they have visited;
- incidents that have occurred at home involving either themselves or other family members;
- significant moments in their lives.

Then invite them to share their lists with a partner. Alternatively, the pupils can each prepare a timeline of the significant events in their lives.

Encourage them to bring in any photographs they may have that were taken at significant moments in their lives or that show places of significance to them. You could get them to show the photos to a partner and to talk about them, before choosing one of the photographs and writing a paragraph about what is in the photo and why it is significant. The photograph and paragraph could be incorporated into a more detailed autobiography (see below).

Another way of getting students to think about important events in their lives is to introduce the idea of thinking about their lives 'alphabiographically'. This involves going through the alphabet and seeing whether a word beginning with that letter sparks off a memory of a particular event. For example, 'A' might trigger a memory of an aunt, of appendicitis, of an accident or an aeroplane flight; 'F' might trigger a memory of being frightened, going fishing, playing football or of a particular friend; and so on. They could draft a paragraph about one of these memories for inclusion in their more detailed autobiographies.

Making a plan

Explain that if they are going to write in detail about themselves, they will need not only to make notes about what they want to include in their autobiography, but to structure their writing by making a plan.

Encourage them to make notes under different headings. Draw a spidergram on the whiteboard with examples of the type of headings they can use:

- My earliest memories
- Where I have lived
- My family
- My interests
- Me
- My schooldays
- A day I'll never forget
- My hopes and ambitions
- A place I'll always remember

When they have made their notes, they can use the headings to plan the order in which they are going to write about themselves and their lives. Explain that the order may depend on the audience for which they are writing. For example, if they were writing to introduce themselves to someone, they might start by writing about their age, describing their appearance and their interests. If they were writing their life story for a magazine and a more general audience, they might start by writing about their family or their earliest memories.

Encourage them to think about a more general audience and to plan the different sections they are going to include by drawing a flow chart.

The students can then draft their autobiographies in sections as if they were writing it for a magazine.

Writing tip: grabbing the audience's attention

Talk about how important the first sentence of a piece of writing is and how, for example, you need to start an autobiographical piece with a sentence that will grab the reader's attention.

Put the following examples on the board of how some students began accounts of their earliest memories and discuss why Ben's is the most effective, because it is the most dramatic, while Alison's is the least effective:

> My earliest memory is of going to playgroup, but I can't remember much about it, except that it was held in a big hall.
>
> (Alison)

> I can't claim to remember being born, but my birth was very dramatic, as I was born on the pavement outside the maternity hospital.
>
> (Ben)

> I was playing in the kitchen and Mum was upstairs. It was a hot day and the kitchen door was open, so I decided to go for a walk.
>
> (Charlie)

I was born in Carlisle on Saturday, 12 October 2002 and we lived in a terraced house until I was three and a half.

(Donna)

Invite the students to write the opening sentences of a paragraph about their earliest memories and then compare them in a class discussion and decide whose grab the reader's attention most effectively.

Revising and redrafting

Use **Activity sheet 1: autobiographical writing** to get the students to practise their skills of drafting and redrafting.

Activity sheet 1: autobiographical writing

Here is the first draft of an account of 'My earliest days' by a student called Waseem:

My earliest days

I was four years old and I was in a nursery. I got angry with another boy and got told off because I hit him on the head with a wooden brick. At the age of three I went to the zoo. I put my finger in a cage. A bird bit me. My mum took me to the First Aid post. I got told off again. Another thing happened when I was four and visiting Pakistan. I got separated from my mum in the market and got lost for an hour.

Discuss Waseem's first draft with a partner and suggest how it could be improved:

- Talk about his opening sentence. Can you suggest a better opening sentence?
- Waseem has not used paragraphs. How could the account be arranged in paragraphs?
- Are the memories presented in the best order?
- Waseem's draft contains a large number of short sentences. Could it be improved by making some of the sentences longer? How would you do this?
- Waseem uses the word 'got' rather a lot. How could you avoid using 'got' so often?
- Could Waseem have included more detail? For example, he doesn't say what the boy did to make him angry. Nor does he describe how his finger was damaged or how he was reunited with his parents.

Imagine you are Waseem. On your own, write a second draft of Waseem's account of his earliest days. As well as using paragraphs, longer sentences and avoiding using 'got', you can make up further details of Waseem's experiences or even include some of your own to make the second draft as interesting as possible. Think carefully about the start and begin with a sentence that grabs the reader's attention.

Compare your version of Waseem's account with your partner's version. Whose version is the most improved? Discuss why.

Assessing autobiographical writing

Ask the children in groups to show each other their detailed autobiographies and to discuss whose autobiography is the most informative, interesting and entertaining. Prompt them, as necessary, to consider the following questions:

1 Do the opening sentences of each section capture the reader's attention?
2 Are the incidents described in chronological order or in a logical sequence? Could the order in which they are described be altered so as to make it more coherent?
3 Are separate paragraphs used for separate incidents?
4 Are the incidents described in sufficient detail? Is there anything else you would like to know about a particular incident?
5 Has the writer used proper sentences?
6 Are the sentences varied? Are there too many short sentences?
7 Are there any grammatical errors?
8 Are there any spelling errors?

Then in a class discussion, ask them to suggest a list of the things they think make a successful piece of autobiographical writing and write the list on the board.

Writing challenge

Ask the children to imagine they are writing about themselves in order to introduce themselves to someone whom they have never met. They are limited to 50 words.

Encourage them to share their introductions in groups and to decide whose introduction contains the most facts and is most successful.

4   Diaries

A diary is a personal record of daily events and of a person's thoughts and feelings.

Explain that people may keep a diary for different reasons. Some people keep a diary to help them express their thoughts and feelings about personal matters. Such diaries are written to be read only by the writer himself or herself. They are similar to the entries that a person might write in a journal (see Chapter 5).

Other people keep a diary to record and comment on the day's events from a personal perspective. These diaries may be read by others beside the person himself or herself, such as family members and friends.

Explain that many such diary entries are written in note form. Put 'A disastrous day' (see below) on the board. Discuss how the person has written notes rather than complete sentences and has only used two connectives ('so' and 'because').

Talk about how the entry differs from how a recount of the day would be written (see Chapter 8). Demonstrate how a recount would be different by getting the pupils to suggest what the first sentences of a recount might be (e.g. 'I overslept so I left the house in a hurry. As a result, I forgot my maths homework.').

Either redraft the rest of the diary entry in complete sentences with the class and write their suggestions on the board or invite individuals to redraft it.

A disastrous day
Overslept. Left the house in a hurry. Forgot my maths homework. Was kept in at playtime to do it all again. Rained all afternoon, so we had PE in the hall instead of football. Got soaked on the way home. Couldn't play my new computer game, because it wouldn't load. Sent to bed early for arguing with my sister. A disastrous day.

Encourage the pupils to keep a diary for a week by giving them some time each day to write their entries in note form. At the end of the week ask them to choose one of the entries and to expand it into a recount.

Writing challenge

Use the ideas presented on **Activity sheet 2: secret diaries** to get the children to write imaginative diary entries.

Activity sheet 2: secret diaries

Here is an extract from 'The secret diary of a young dragon':

> I had a great day at school. First, we had fire-breathing and I came first, because I managed to blow eight smoke rings. Then we had fighting practice and Firesnorter was my partner. We knocked out Thunderflash, who was pretending to be Sir Prancealot and captured his horse. We were chasing after Lightning, who was also pretending to be a knight, and would have caught him, but we ran out of time.

Write the rest of the young dragon's entry for the day. You could describe what the dragon had for lunch, what he did in the flying lesson they had that afternoon and what he did when he got home from school, for example what computer game he played and what programmes he watched on TV.

Write diary entries for the secret diary of an imaginary creature or person:

- the secret diary of a wizard or a witch;
- the secret diary of a ghost or an elf;
- the secret diary of a giant or a troll.

Imagine you are a pet animal and write two contrasting diary entries describing a good day in the pet's life and a bad day; for example, the day when a dog has an adventure because it runs off when being taken for a walk or the day when a dog wakes up to find it has lost its bark.

Curriculum opportunities

In a religious education lesson, you can tell the children a story from the Bible and invite them to imagine they were present and witnessed the events. They can then write a recount of the events in the form of a diary entry.

As part of a history topic, the pupils can imagine what the life of a person would have been like and write a diary entry about their life. For example, they can write the diary entry of a knight who went on a Crusade, a sailor who sailed around the world with Sir Francis Drake or of a Roman soldier on Hadrian's Wall.

Groups of abler readers can study *Zlata's Diary* by Zlata Filipović about life in Sarajevo during its siege. They can then write fictional diary entries describing what it would be like to be a child living in a city during a civil war.

Discuss with pupils who are reading *The Diary of a Wimpy Kid* how the author uses pictures as well as words to tell the story. Invite the pupils to write an extra chapter for the book, using pictures and words in the way that Jeff Kinney does.

The pupils can write about themselves for a specific audience. Instead of writing it as just a personal record, they can write a series of diary entries to be read by someone who lives in another part of the country or in another country, for example in a partnership school. Encourage them to select things to record in their entries that will give the reader a clear idea of who they are, the life they lead, their interests, thoughts and feelings and descriptions of their home, family and school. They could put their diary entries onto the computer and produce a booklet to send to another school.

When studying another country, the pupils can research what life would be like growing up in that country. They can then imagine they are a child living in that country and write a diary entry describing a day in their life.

5 Journals

Explain that a journal is a record of a person's thoughts and feelings.

Getting children to write entries in a journal is a good way of developing the confidence of struggling writers, especially if they know that their writing will not be formally assessed. It gives them the opportunity to choose what they want to write about and to develop their skills of self-expression without having to worry about whether or not their work is going to reach a satisfactory standard.

Introduce the idea of journal writing. Explain that you can use a journal as a record of events, in the same way as you use a diary, or you can use it to express your thoughts and feelings. Tell the children that you will set aside times during the week for journal writing and that they can write about whatever they choose. Stress that you will not be assessing what they write, although you will read what they have written and discuss it with them.

Some children who are confident writers will find it easy enough to choose for themselves what to write, but others will need prompting. At the start of a journal-writing session you can choose an idea or topic from the list below to suggest what they might write about.

When you read a pupil's journal, do not mark it as you would any other piece of writing. Instead, write a comment, which is a response to the ideas the pupil expresses. Invite them to write a response to your comment if they would like to do so.

Ideas and topics for journal writing

An issue I feel strongly about

A person whom I admire

Describe a time when you did something which you later felt ashamed of doing

What changes you would make if children ran the school?

If you could travel through time what age would you go to?

If you could be someone else who would you be?

The best way to get rid of anger is ...

What makes me feel sad

How I feel about brothers and sisters

If you had three wishes, what would you wish for?

What makes a good friend?

Sometimes it's better to lie than tell the truth

My ambition is ...

The most courageous person I know

Two wrongs don't make a right

The thing that concerns me most about the future is ...

Children should always be consulted about important family matters

A time I was embarrassed

The strangest thing that has happened to me

6   Letters

A letter is a piece of writing which is addressed to a person or an organisation and usually delivered by post or e-mail.

Discuss the different reasons why people write letters and e-mails – to tell each other about events that have happened in their lives, to make enquiries, to convey information, to make a complaint, to express an opinion.

Explain the difference between informal letters, which are personal and which may be chatty in style, and formal letters, such as letters to a newspaper expressing an opinion (see Chapter 12) and letters of complaint (see below), which have a business-like style and tone. This chapter focuses on formal letters, while the chapter on messages (Chapter 7) focuses on informal messages, such as text messages, e-mails and letters.

Use **Activity sheet 3: a letter of complaint** which contains a formal letter to a local council complaining about the condition of a play area in a local park.

Writing tip: avoid inappropriate language

Give pairs a copy of the activity sheet. Talk about the difference between the informal language they use to speak to each other in the playground and the formal language they use when talking to people in more formal situations, for example when talking to the headteacher or school secretary. Explain that just as it is inappropriate to use playground language when talking in the school office, it is inappropriate to use informal expressions in formal letters. Ask the pupils in pairs to study the letter of complaint and to choose which phrases are more formal and, therefore, more appropriate in a formal letter.

Activity sheet 3: a letter of complaint

26 Parkside Crescent
Northtown NR6 7RQ

Councillor Greaves
Town Hall
Northtown NR99 6OX

30 January 2013

Dear Councillor Greaves

I'd like to / I am writing to complain about **the awful state / the unsafe condition** of the play area **in Parkside Crescent / at the bottom of our road**.

The swings have been **smashed / vandalised** and a lot of the other equipment has been **damaged / wrecked**, so **it needs to be repaired / you should get it repaired**.

As well as all that / In addition there is the problem of broken bottles. **I think someone / I reckon someone** will get badly cut if nothing is done about it.

What's more / Moreover ,the litter bins are always **crammed full / overflowing** so there's litter everywhere. **Can't you do something / Is it possible** to arrange for them to be emptied more regularly?

And another thing / Also there is **dog muck / dog poo** all over the field. **It's disgusting / It's a health hazard. What gets me / What concerns me** is that dog owners seem to think **it's no big deal / it's not their problem**.

I want to know / Please can you let me know what you can do **to improve the condition of the play area / to get things sorted out**.

Yours sincerely

Jessica Hart

In pairs, study the letter. Discuss the phrases that are in bold. Choose the ones that are more appropriate in a formal letter, then cross out the ones that are inappropriate because they use informal language.

A formal letter

Ask the children to imagine they have bought a computer game or a piece of computer equipment that is faulty. They could either think of a game or piece of equipment themselves or refer to a catalogue, such as the Dell catalogue, to find an appropriate item. Get them to draft a letter of complaint specifying what is wrong and asking for either a refund or a replacement. Remind them that it is important to use formal language and to lay the letter out properly. Use Activity sheet 3 to show pupils the layout of a formal letter and discuss where to put the addresses, the date and the greeting, and how to end the letter.

Write a letter to King Arthur applying for a job as a knight. Explain what qualities you possess that make you a suitable candidate for the job.

Curriculum opportunities

You can involve the children in the planning of a class outing, related to their topic. They can draft formal e-mails or letters, for example to a local place of interest, enquiring about what happens during the day and about how much it costs and how to book places. The contents of such letters will depend on the place to be visited.

They can then draft a letter to a bus company enquiring about the cost of hiring a coach, and a letter to parents informing them of the trip.

Before they draft each of the letters, discuss with them what are the key questions they need to ask in their enquiries and what key information they need to include in their letters to parents.

After they have drafted the letters, ask groups to share their drafts and to discuss whose letter is the best because it not only contains the necessary details, but also because it is written in a formal style and uses appropriate language.

After the pupils have been on a visit, for example to a local place of interest or to an activity centre, they can write a letter of thanks to the guide or the instructor.

Similarly, after they have been given a talk by a visitor, such as a writer, or taken part in an art project or music project, they can write a letter of thanks to the visitor.

Writing challenge

Invite the pupils to write a formal letter which uses inappropriate language. They could write a letter from a teacher to a parent inviting them to come to the school to discuss their son's or daughter's behaviour, for example their failure to be punctual, to wear the correct uniform, to do their homework, to pay attention in class or to behave properly in the playground.

Either they could think of their own opening or begin the letter as follows:

Hi Johnno's dad and mum

How are you doing guys?

7　Messages

Messages are short pieces of writing that can be exchanged over the internet by computers and by devices such as mobile phones, iPhones, iPads and iPods.

Writing messages

Explain that there are several types of message you can send electronically over the internet. You can send messages to your friends by e-mail or chat to them on social networking sites, such as Facebook. You can send text messages to your friends on your mobile phone.

Explain that text messaging is a very informal way of communicating and that in order to keep text messages short, lots of abbreviations are used and punctuation is largely ignored. This is acceptable when you are texting your friends or chatting to them.

However, it is not appropriate to use abbreviations and to ignore punctuation in most types of writing. You will lose marks if you ignore punctuation and use abbreviations in written answers in tests or examinations.

Chatting in txtspk

Talk about how people use SMS language or txtspk when chatting to a friend. Point out the different methods that are used in txtspk to abbreviate words:

1   Single letters are used instead of words: u for you, y for why and c for see or sea.
2   Numbers are used for words or parts of words that sound like the word, e.g. 2 for to/two/too, 4 for for/four/fore and gr8 for great, l8 for late and 6t for sixty.
3   Words are shortened by leaving out the vowels, e.g. smmr for summer, wntr for winter, hsptl for hospital, or by leaving out strings of letters, e.g. hwk for homework.
4   Slang terms are used because they are shorter than the conventional words, e.g. soz for sorry, coz for because.
5   Words are spelt as they are pronounced, e.g. wiv for with and ule for you'll.
6   Phrases are shortened into acronyms – a word formed from the initial letters of a group of words – or into easily recognisable groups of letters, e.g. bbs be back soon, gtg got to go, lol laugh out loud.

Use **Activity sheet 4: do u no ur txtspk?**, which consists of an activity in which pupils have to write the abbreviations that are used in txtspk for commonly used words and phrases.

Activity sheet 4: do u no ur txtspk?

Write the abbreviations that are used in txtspk for each of these words and phrases:

Anyone

Are you

Be back soon

Before

Bye for now

Don't be late

For your information

Got to go

Great

I don't know

Just a second

Laugh out loud

Oh my gosh

Please

See you later

Take care

Thanks

Welcome back

Why

You're welcome

Update your status

Discuss how people often use texts to update their status – to let their friends or family know where they are and what they are doing. Another common use of text messages is to make arrangements. Here are some situations in which a person would need to text an urgent message updating their status. Ask individuals to choose one of the situations and write the message that they would text.

- You were flying in a private plane which has crash-landed in a jungle. You are the only survivor.
- You and a companion are climbing a mountain when you are trapped by a blizzard.
- You are a spy and you are on your way to meet an informant in a park, when you suddenly realise you are walking into a trap.
- You wake up in a strange room with a locked door and no windows.
- You are separated from your companions while exploring some caves.
- You are out at sea in a motor-boat which runs out of fuel.
- You are walking across a moor when you fall down an old mineshaft.

As a follow-up, they can write a tweet to let people know that they are safe and explaining how they were rescued.

Explain that text messages can also be used to inform your family and friends of good news, to send out an invitation or as a way of saying thank you. Ask them to imagine that you have some good news to tell your family and friends. Choose one of these situations and write the message that you would text:

- Your team won the final and you scored the winner.
- You won first prize in a competition.
- You have been auditioned for a part in a movie and have been offered it.
- You have been chosen to go on a trip into space.

Write the text that you would send out as an invitation to a party of some kind. Use the checklist in the chapter on invitations to make sure you include all the important details (see Chapter 20).

Encourage them to think about what they are going to do at the weekend and to text a friend offering to meet them and do something together.

Write a thank you text to a cousin who has sent you £10 for your birthday.

Ask them to imagine that two children have discovered what appears to be a cache of stolen goods hidden in a disused warehouse. They decide to keep the warehouse under surveillance to see what is going on. One of them is watching the front gate, one the back entrance. Write the texts they send to each other.

Curriculum opportunities

You can explain how people used to send urgent messages by telegram. You could show them examples of telegrams and ask them to rewrite the telegrams as text messages.

As part of a history topic they can send text messages home from sailors involved in famous voyages of discovery, from explorers who took part in epic journeys or from soldiers who took part in invasions, such as the Viking and Roman invasions of Britain.

8   Recounts

A recount is an account of an event. It may be an account of a personal experience or the retelling of a factual event or incident.

Explain that the purpose of a recount is to retell events, such as an account of a personal experience. It may take the form of an account of a day's events, for example of a visit to a museum, and may be part of an autobiography, a letter or a journal or diary entry.

Discuss how a recount always has the same features. Put **Activity sheet 5: a great day out** on the board.

Point out that it consists of an introductory paragraph, followed by a number of paragraphs which present the events in chronological order, and that there is a final concluding paragraph. Invite the pupils to draw a timeline of what Pam's family did in order to show how the events are described in sequence.

Talk about how Pam uses time connectives to link the events and make a list on the board of the ones she uses.

Talk about how Pam includes some powerful words – the adjectives 'vicious' and 'spindly', and verbs such as 'roaming', 'gobbling' and 'waddling'. Discuss how she avoids the tired word 'interesting', using 'fascinating' instead.

As the follow-up to a class outing, ask the children to draft a recount of the day. Remind them that the events should be recounted chronologically and put a list of time connectives on the board for them to refer to as they write (e.g. first, next, after, afterwards, then, soon, when, meanwhile, later, eventually, finally).

Writing tip: avoid 'nothing sentences'

Explain that when you are writing a recount, you can easily fall into the trap of writing 'nothing sentences'. These are sentences that are either vague or that include insignificant details. For example, if you begin an account of a day out by writing, 'I got up and got dressed, then I went downstairs and had my breakfast', you are not saying anything significant about your day out.

Discuss how Pam mostly includes only the important things they did, but point out that the final sentence of the first paragraph could have been left out, as it deals with insignificant details. Also, the final sentence of the fourth paragraph is a 'nothing sentence'.

Similarly, point out that putting 'and so on' or 'etc.' adds nothing to a sentence, because it is too vague. For example, the sentence 'In the adventure playground, we went on the swings, slides, etc.' tells you nothing except that they went on the swings and the slides.

Before they redraft their accounts, encourage them in pairs to use **Assessing recounts: a checklist** to think critically about each other's drafts and to write down their suggestions as to how their drafts could be improved. Then get them to redraft their accounts. End by sharing some of their accounts in a whole-class discussion.

Activity sheet 5: a great day out

A great day out

On Saturday, it was my birthday and we went to the Cotswold Wildlife Park for the day. It took us about an hour to drive there and we arrived there shortly after the park opened. Dad paid for us to get in and we parked the car. We got out of the car and got ready to set off.

First, we saw some birds, including a vulture, which had a vicious beak. Then we went on a train which took us right round the park, so we could see the animals that were roaming in their enclosures such as deer and rhinos.

By then it was 11 o'clock and we went to meet the giraffes. I was surprised at how tall they were and how spindly their legs were. A keeper told us all about where they lived and what they ate, which was fascinating.

Afterwards we had a picnic on the lawn outside the big house. My brother and I went on the adventure play area. There were all kinds of things to play on.

Next we did brass rubbing. I thought it might be boring, but it was fun. My brother did a brass rubbing of a leopard and I did one of a tiger.

We then went to look at the plants, which was boring! But after that we had an ice-cream.

Finally, we saw the keepers feed the penguins. There was this one penguin who was really greedy. He kept diving in the pool and gobbling up the fish. He even went waddling after the keeper when the bucket was empty.

It was a great day out. I thoroughly enjoyed it and I learnt a lot about the animals we saw.

(Pam)

Assessing recounts: a checklist

1 Is there a clear introduction which tells the reader clearly what the account is about, and when and where the events took place?
2 Are separate paragraphs used for separate events?
3 Are the events recounted in time order (chronological order)?
4 Are the sentence openings varied?
5 Have time connectives, such as first, next, after, afterwards, when, later on, meanwhile, finally, been used to link the events?
6 Is the account written in the past tense?
7 Does the account focus on the important events, including relevant details?
8 Does it include any unimportant details that could be left out?
9 Does the account use powerful verbs and descriptive adjectives?
10 Is there a conclusion with a personal comment about the event?

Write a comment on the account, saying what its good points are and how the writer could improve it when it is being redrafted.

Writing challenge

Invite them to write a recount of a day at the seaside or at a theme park when everything went wrong. Give them a word limit of 100 words. How many things can they describe going wrong within 100 words?

Curriculum opportunities

There are many opportunities for writing recounts during history topics. Children can imagine, for example, that they were present and witnessed a historical event, such as the Fire of London, or a battle, such as the Battle of Hastings. They can write a recount describing the event. Alternatively, they can write a recount of a day in the life of a person, such as a Roman soldier or an Anglo-Saxon villager.

Part Two

Persuasive writing

9   Advertisements

The purpose of an advertisement is to persuade people to buy a particular product or service or to inform people about an event.

Explain that while advertisements for products and services provide you with information about the product or service, their main aim is to persuade you to buy that product or service.

For sale advertisements

Talk about how people often sell things they no longer need by putting an advert in a shop window or the classified advertisements column of a newspaper.

Use **Activity sheet 6: classified adverts**. Study the three advertisements from the *Witches and Wizards Weekly*. Discuss how the writers try to make the things they have for sale attractive and worth buying. Pick out the key words and phrases they use to try to persuade people to buy them. Then invite the children to write similar short advertisements.

Activity sheet 6: classified adverts

Here are three adverts from the *Witches and Wizards Weekly*.

House-trained dragons

Make excellent children's pets.

All colours.

Also ideal as alternatives to barbecues and central heating.

Phone Firesnorter 084 084 or text DRAGS4U.

To let

One room hovel.

With fully fitted stove and cauldron. Bat-infested.

Would suit apprentice wizard.

Contact Slumits Estate Agents, Low Street, Magichester.

For sale

Complete set of *Magica Suprema*.

Mint condition. Signed by the author.

Will consider part-exchange for medieval wand.

Contact Professor Skumble, The Dark Tower WW14.

Write an advertisement for something you have for sale, such as a broomstick, a wand, a book of recipes for spells, a crystal or a phial of potion. Remember that when you are placing an advert in a magazine or newspaper, the more words you use the more you will have to pay, so keep your advert short and clear – a maximum of 25 words.

Put the following advertisement for a shed to let on the board:

> Vacant – one shed. Would suit a gang of four children.
>
> Well hidden behind bushes, at the rear of 41 Oak Avenue, this disused shed would be ideal as a hideout and perfect for secret meetings. Appropriately furnished with scrounged bits of carpet and an old deck-chair or two, it would be a comfortable refuge from interfering grown-ups and tiresome younger brothers and eminently suitable for picnics and councils of war. With easy access from 41's back garden via a broken fence-panel, the shed is conveniently situated on a route to the stream and the recreation ground.

Discuss how the shed is made to seem attractive to children. Focus on the phrases the writer uses to make the shed seem a good place for a group of children to meet, such as 'ideal as a hideout', 'perfect for secret meetings', 'a comfortable refuge', 'eminently suitable', 'with easy access' and 'conveniently situated'.

Writing challenge

Invite the children to imagine the school buildings are for sale. What features would they highlight? What sort of buyer would they try to attract? How might the buildings be converted? Encourage them to be imaginative. Would it make a good home for older people? A millionaire's mansion? A prison?

Individually or in pairs get them to draft their 'For sale' adverts describing the school buildings, then form groups to share their adverts and to discuss whose is the most effective advert and why.

Writing tip: use adjectives to make it sound attractive

Either download some descriptions of holiday destinations and holiday hotels from the internet sites of holiday companies or obtain some holiday brochures from a travel company. Study the advertisements describing a number of resorts and focus on the adjectives that are used to describe them and make them sound special. Build up a list of adjectives used in advertising and put it on the word wall. Encourage the children to add to the list.

Words you could include are: wonderful, magnificent, spectacular, stunning, amazing, extraordinary, sensational, remarkable, astounding, luxurious, incredible, phenomenal, astonishing, splendid, superb, excellent, exceptional.

Use **Activity sheet 7: holiday advertisements** to get individuals to draft their own holiday advertisements.

Activity sheet 7: holiday advertisements

In pairs, study this advertisement for a holiday at the Panorama Beach Hotel. Notice how each sentence addresses the reader directly by starting with a verb. Pick out the adjectives that are used in order to make the hotel seem attractive. Discuss the use the writer makes of alliteration in the description.

The Panorama Beach Hotel

Enjoy the holiday of a lifetime at the exotic Panorama Beach Hotel. Have breakfast on the balcony with stunning views of the ocean. Top up your tan as you laze on a lounger, listening to the whisper of the waves or take a stroll along the beautiful, soft, sandy beach. Swim in the sparkling sea or one of our three magnificent pools. Dine in style at our luxurious five-star restaurant or enjoy a romantic meal beneath the stars at our beach-front Tables for Two. Book now for a fabulous holiday you'll never forget.

The advertisement for the Panorama Beach Hotel is aimed at adults. Write a description of a holiday which is aimed at children rather than adults. Either think up your own name or write an advertisement for Paradise Park beginning, 'Children will be in paradise at Paradise Park'.

Write a spoof advertisement for a holiday at a guesthouse at Sludge-on-Sea: 'For a holiday you'll want to forget, stay at the Grim Guesthouse, Sludge-on-Sea ...'

Study the brochures for a theme park, such as Alton Towers, or an adventure park, such as Go Ape! Write an advertisement for a theme park.

Writing slogans

Explain that a slogan is a short distinctive phrase used by advertisers which is designed to be memorable. Give examples of successful slogans, such as 'Finger lickin' good' (Kentucky Fried Chicken) and 'Live in your world. Play in ours' (PlayStation 2).

Get the children to share slogans that they know from TV adverts and magazine adverts.

Discuss the features of a good slogan. Talk about how it needs to be short and snappy, so a slogan is usually a phrase, rather than a complete sentence. Mention how a slogan will often have a rhythm to it. Remind them what alliteration is – the use of several words together that all begin with the same letter or sound – and point out how it is used in a slogan such as 'Barney's Beefburgers Best for Barbecues'. Or they may use rhyme: 'The sweet that's a treat.'

Slogans also sometimes use humour in the form of puns. Remind the children what a pun is – the use of a word or phrase in order to create ambiguity. For example, 'Brilliant cleaning starts with Finish' (Finish washing-up powder), 'Do me a Quaver' (Quavers snack) or a made-up slogan for a new brand of trainers: 'Look sharp in Sharpies.'

As a whole class, ask them to produce slogans for Funchies, a new kind of breakfast cereal; Lickit, a new lollipop; Fizz, a new drink; Gleam, a new toothpaste; and the SpeedStar, a new bicycle.

Some slogans that you could suggest are: 'Funchies – the Crunchy Way to Start the Day'; 'Lickit – You'll Like a Lickit a Lot'; 'Get Fizzical'; 'Give your teeth a Gleamclean'; and 'Speedsters Go Faster on SpeedStars'.

Invite individuals to make up a slogan for a new product, such as a new skateboard, new trainers or a new computer game.

Curriculum opportunities

As part of a technology project, for example, in which the children are asked to design and make a toy, such as a glove puppet, they can produce an advert for the toy to go in a catalogue.

10 Arguments

A piece of writing which expresses a point of view on an issue, giving reasons to support that opinion, is called an argument.

Explain that written arguments express a point of view in such forms as essays, articles in newspapers and magazines, and letters to newspapers and magazines.

Talk about how a written argument needs to present the reasons for having that point of view and that a good argument will contain evidence to support that viewpoint.

As a starter, give individuals or pairs five minutes in which to list one of the following:

five good reasons why children should be allowed to choose their own bedtime;

five good reasons why children should wear what they like to school;

five good reasons why we should have longer holidays.

Explain that a balanced argument not only puts the reasons *for* supporting that viewpoint but will also put the arguments *against* that viewpoint.

Draw two columns on the board labelled 'For' and 'Against'. Ask some of the pupils to read out their reasons *for* being allowed to choose their own bedtime, to wear what they like to school or to have longer holidays, and list them on the board. Then encourage them to suggest the reasons that people might argue *against* that view and write their suggestions on the board.

Use **Activity sheet 8: writing an argument** to explain that a written argument follows a set pattern.

Point out other features of the text:

- how arguments are written in the present tense;
- how the writer tries to involve the reader by writing using the first person plural, referring to 'we' and 'us';
- how the writer asks a question in order to reinforce her argument;
- how the writer uses connectives that emphasise and help to persuade ('surely', 'however') and that introduce evidence ('for example').

Writing tip: vary your sentence openings

Focus on the use of connectives in argument writing by making copies of **Activity sheet 9: persuasive sentence starters** and discussing how they can use particular sentence starters to sequence their arguments, to express and emphasise their opinions, and to provide evidence which illustrates the points they are making.

The pupils can then draft their own arguments on the issue you have been discussing, referring to the sheet to select openings for their sentences and reminding themselves of the arguments for and against the issue by referring to the lists on the board.

Pupils in pairs can then use **Assessing arguments: a checklist** to assess their drafts. Encourage them to identify what their partner has done successfully as well as to make suggestions as to what they might do to improve their drafts.

They can then redraft their arguments and show the revised version to their partner, pointing out the changes they have made.

Encourage the children to express their opinions by having a 'Viewpoints noticeboard' to which members of the class can contribute their views. Invite pairs or groups of children to take it in turns to choose a discussion topic for the week. This can be either a school issue, such as what charity should the school choose to support as its charity of the year, a local issue, such as plans to close a swimming pool, or an issue that is in the news, such as should all police officers carry guns. The members of the class can then post their views on the 'Viewpoints noticeboard'.

Activity sheet 8: writing an argument

Written arguments follow a set pattern. The first paragraph is an introduction stating the main argument. There are then a series of paragraphs giving reasons which support the point of view expressed in the main argument. There is a final paragraph which is a conclusion summarising the author's point of view.

My views on homework

Paragraph 1: a statement introducing the main argument and your point of view
Children should not be expected to do so much homework. We get homework every night. Surely that's too much.

Paragraph 2: the first reason for your point of view
We spend six hours at school every day, but when we get home we're expected to do more schoolwork. Why can't we do everything we need to do at school?

Paragraph 3: the second reason for your point of view
Having homework means we have less time to play. For example, on Tuesdays when I go to ballet and on Thursdays when I go to judo, I have no time left for myself.

Paragraph 4: the third reason for your point of view
Teachers and parents say homework is good for you. However, a lot of the time all you have to do is to repeat what you learned in school by filling in a worksheet.

Paragraph 5: a concluding statement summarising your point of view
Finally, we don't have a choice about whether or not we do homework. I think that we should have less homework and it should be voluntary.

Assessing arguments: a checklist

1 Is there an opening statement which clearly states the main argument and point of view?
2 Are the reasons for the point of view presented in separate paragraphs?
3 Is there a conclusion summarising the writer's viewpoint?
4 Is the argument balanced? Does it include reasons why the writer disagrees with people who have a different point of view?
5 Is the argument written in the present tense?
6 Are the sentence openings varied?
7 Are any questions used to reinforce the argument?
8 Are connectives used that might help to persuade the reader?
9 Is any use made of pronouns, such as 'you', 'we' or 'us', to try to involve the reader?
10 Has the writer avoided including any 'nothing sentences', which don't really add anything to the argument?

© 2014, *Let's Write*, John Foster, Routledge

Activity sheet 9: persuasive sentence starters

When you are writing an argument, you need to vary your sentence openings. These lists give examples of different types of sentence starters you can use.

Sentence starters that you can use to sequence an argument:

- Firstly ...
- For a start ...
- Secondly ...
- Thirdly ...
- Finally ...
- In conclusion ...

Sentence starters that you can use to express opinions:

- It would appear that ...
- It seems that ...
- In my opinion ...
- Some people think that ...
- On the other hand ...
- Moreover ...
- However ...
- In spite of ...
- Therefore ...

Sentence starters that you can use to emphasise the points you are making:

- This clearly shows that ...
- Isn't it obvious ...
- Surely ...
- Everybody knows that ...
- The fact is ...
- If only ...
- Most people agree that ...
- Why can't people see that ...
- Naturally, I feel strongly that ...
- More importantly ...

Sentence starters that you can use to provide evidence that illustrates your argument:

- For example ...
- For instance ...
- Here are two reasons why ...
- We can see from the evidence that ...
- In other words ...

© 2014, *Let's Write*, John Foster, Routledge

Writing challenge

Invite the pupils to try to write a convincing argument in less than 60 words. They can either choose their own subject or one from the list (below):

Why children should be paid to come to school

Why there should be free lunches for everybody

Why the school holidays should be longer

11 Blurbs

A blurb is a piece of writing that appears on the back cover of a book. Its aim is to whet the reader's appetite so that they will want to buy the book and read it.

Explain that a good blurb will contain a summary of what the book contains. If the book is a novel, it will give a summary of the story, without giving too much away about the plot and the ending. If the book is a non-fiction book, it will summarise the contents. If it is a poetry book, it will tell you about the poems that are to be found in the book.

A blurb will also aim to promote the book, so it will use adjectives that are designed to capture the reader's attention and make the book sound interesting.

Focus on a book you have recently used with the class and discuss the blurb. Does the blurb make the book sound interesting?

Use **Activity sheet 10: blurbs** and discuss how the writers have attempted to make the books sound interesting. Pick out the key words they have chosen and talk about how they use alliteration. Point out that because space is limited on a book's cover, a blurb has to be short and snappy, and that consequently the writers may not always write complete sentences.

Writing tip: use alliteration

Explain that many blurbs use alliteration to try to capture the reader's attention in the way that advertising slogans do (see Chapter 9). Remind the pupils what alliteration is and point out how it is used to describe Louis Sachar's book as 'fantastically funny' and the contents of John Foster's book – 'teasing tongue-twisters, ridiculous riddles, loopy limericks, batty booklists, dotty definitions'.

Work with the class to produce alliterative phrases that they might use in blurbs to describe a book as exciting or full of excitement (e.g. 'exceptionally exciting', 'extremely exciting', 'exquisitely exciting', 'excellent excitement', 'especially exciting').

Then ask them to suggest alliterative phrases to describe a book as humorous (e.g. 'hilarious humour'), informative (e.g. 'immensely informative'), full of suspense (e.g. 'spine-chilling suspense') or thrilling (e.g. 'a terrifying thriller').

Make a list of alliterative phrases to use in blurbs and put it on display. Get the children to add any alliterative phrases that they find in the blurbs of books in the class library.

Get the children to look critically at the blurb on a book they have read recently. Does it promote the book effectively? Does it give an accurate description of what the book is about? Does it focus on the key character and the key feature of the plot? Does it give away too much of the story? Invite them to write an alternative blurb. Then discuss with them how their blurb is different and why.

Curriculum opportunities

As part of a poetry project, invite the children to make their own anthologies of their favourite poems. Encourage them to group the poems within the book, for example by topics, authors or types of poems. Get them to draw up a contents list and index, to think of a title, to design a cover and to write a blurb.

Activity sheet 10: blurbs

Blurb 1:

There has been a terrible mistake and Wayside School has been built all wrong! The classrooms were meant to be in a row and now they are on top of each other. All 30 of them. Maybe that is why strange things happen at Wayside School ...

   In this fantastically funny book get ready to meet the meanest teacher ever, Mrs Gorf, and terrible Todd who always gets sent home, John who can only read upside down and all the other eccentric and wonderful children, and teachers, in this crazy mixed-up school.

Sideways Stories from Wayside School
By Louis Sachar (Bloomsbury Children's Books)

Blurb 2:

Warning! Contains pirates,

Vikings, ghosts, vampires

and flesh-eating zombies!

Come inside for hilarious jokes and rhymes,

as well as teasing tongue-twisters,

ridiculous riddles, loopy limericks, batty booklists,

dotty definitions and much, much more.

YOU'LL DIE LAUGHING!

How Do You Make a Skeleton Laugh?
Compiled by John Foster (Oxford University Press)

12   Letters expressing an opinion

Explain that letters, such as a letter to a newspaper or a letter to the school council, can be used to put forward an argument and express an opinion about an issue.

Use **Activity sheet 11: in my opinion**.

Ask groups to study the four letters which were entered for a competition in which children were asked to write a letter on an issue which concerned them. Imagine they were judging the competition. Which letter would win first prize?

Prompt groups to consider points such as:

- Which letter has the most effective opening?
- In which letter is the main statement best supported by the arguments developed and the evidence quoted?
- In which letter is the order of the arguments developed most clearly paragraph by paragraph?
- Which letter has the most effective ending?
- Which of the letters adopts the right tone, using only formal language and avoiding informal language?
- Which letter involves the reader most effectively?

Hold a class discussion in which each group explains which letter they chose as the winner and why. Then take a vote to decide which letter the class would choose.

Invite the children to draft their own letters to a newspaper on an issue which they feel strongly about. Then, in groups, encourage them to assess each other's letters and to suggest how they might be redrafted and improved.

Ask the children to imagine that a former governor of the school has died and left £5000 to the school on condition that the children must decide how the money is to be spent. In pairs or groups, ask the children to list their ideas of how the money should be spent. Then draw up a list of their suggestions. Prompt them, as necessary, with suggestions about things that the school needs, which they might not suggest – such as a new school library or for the old school hall to be refurbished.

Invite them to discuss the ideas in groups, arguing the cases for and against the various suggestions. Then ask them individually to write a letter to the governors saying what they think the money should be spent on and why.

Assessing letters which express opinions

Encourage the children to use this checklist to assess their letters.

- Does the opening grab the reader's attention? Can you suggest a better opening?
- Is the main argument clearly stated in the opening paragraph?

- Are paragraphs used properly? Could the structure of the letter be improved, for example by altering the order in which the points are made?
- Do the arguments and evidence quoted support the main statement? Are the arguments fully developed? Are there any other points that the writer could have made?
- Is the ending effective? Could it be improved, and if so how?
- Has the writer used only formal language and avoided using informal expressions which are inappropriate in a formal letter?

Activity sheet 11: in my opinion

In groups, study these four letters which were entries for a competition in which children were asked to write a letter to a newspaper about an issue which concerned them. Decide which of the letters you would choose as the winner. Then share your views in a class discussion.

Computer geeks

I think it's ridiculous the way boys spend so much time playing computer games. They are a waste of time and money. They spend all their time shooting monsters and zapping aliens.

All they can talk about is what level they are on and who's got the highest score. It's so boring!!! They should try reading a book some time. And the prices they pay for the games are ridiculous too. They are just a bunch of geeks.

(Alyson)

Dangers of cycling

I've just been out on my new bike and realised how dangerous cycling can be. I was going to start cycling to and from school, but now I'm not so sure it's a good idea, as I'd have to go round a busy roundabout.

I am shocked about the way drivers treat cyclists in this country. Drivers, especially lorry drivers, cut you up as if they can't see you. I was nearly knocked off my bike by a container lorry which pulled over right in front of me.

Cycle lanes are a good idea, but there aren't enough of them. No wonder people start riding on the pavement. But pedestrians can be really nasty if you do. There was one man who gave me a right telling off when I rang my bell to warn him I was coming.

Mind you there are some cyclists who don't realise how dangerous it is. They whizz out of their driveways across the pavement into the street. It's a wonder there aren't more accidents.

(Kim)

Rubbish

Why are our towns and countryside so full of litter?

We went on holiday to Austria last year and the thing that struck me most about the country is that even in the main cities there was no litter in the street. But our streets are full of litter.

People say they are worried about the environment. If they really cared, they wouldn't drop their litter or throw it out of their car windows. The mess that's left outside our local McDonald's is just one example.

And another thing, recycling is a good idea. But not everyone uses their recycling containers properly. I think people who still put rubbish that could be recycled into their bins ought to be fined.

Our environment's precious. We need to look after it.

(Sunil)

Sun tans

It's absurd the lengths some people will go to in order to get a sun tan. I recently went to Spain and there were people who spent all day lying in the sun.

You lie around getting hot, sweaty and uncomfortable. You end up looking like a lobster and feeling extremely sore, unable to sleep at night because you are sunburnt.

And what happens after this self-inflicted torture? You go brown for a couple of days, then your skin starts to peel.

One of my friends, whose family originally came from the West Indies, thinks it really strange that white people spend so much time trying to make their skin brown.

Then, there's the danger of spending too much time in the sun and getting skin cancer. Lying in the sun all day in order to get a tan is not only a waste of time, but a risk to your health.

(Gemma)

Writing challenge

In 20 minutes draft a letter to a famous person in order to persuade them to support a charity event which you are organising.

Curriculum opportunities

When you are studying the local environment, the pupils can write letters to the local newspaper expressing their views on what could be done to improve the local area. Prompt them to consider points such as the condition of the roads and pavements, the amount of litter and graffiti, local playgrounds and parks, transport services and other community services such as a community centre, health centre, library and youth centre.

In a Personal, Social, Health and Economic Education (PSHEE) session, talk to the children about the work of Amnesty International. Encourage the pupils to use the internet to find out about Amnesty's letter-writing campaigns and to draft letters to the government of a country about a particular child or children whose human rights are being violated.

13 Reviews

Explain that a review has two purposes. First, it aims to give the reader information. If it is a review of a novel, it will aim to tell you something about the theme of the story. If it is a review of a non-fiction book, it will aim to tell you what features of the subject it covers. Similarly, a review of a film or CD will describe its contents and a review of a computer game will tell you what sort of game it is.

The second purpose of a review is to give the reviewer's personal opinion – to say what he or she liked or disliked about the book, film, CD or game. The reader can then decide whether or not it is a book they'd like to read, a film they'd like to see or a game they'd like to buy.

Book reviews

Hand out copies of **Activity sheet 12: planning a review of a novel** and encourage the pupils to write their own book reviews either of a novel they have recently read or of a novel by one of the following authors: Roald Dahl, Jacqueline Wilson, Michael Morpurgo, Lemony Snicket, Eoin Colfer, Anthony Horovitz.

Writing tip: avoid giving the plot away

Talk about how it is important to give the reader an idea of who the main characters are and what happens in the book without revealing any crucial bits of the plot. Discuss how they can focus on the theme of the novel and what type of story it is without going into detail that will give the plot away.

Read them Evie's review (below) and talk about how she manages to say what the book is about and what she liked about it without giving away too much of the plot.

> *Atticus Claw Breaks the Law* **by Jennifer Gray, reviewed by Evie Casmore**
> This was a really great book. The story is about a very particular crime and a strange place where it took place. I really liked the book as there was lots going on all the time. The best bit of the book was when Toffly's tiara was going to be stolen by a magpie! It got very exciting. My favourite character was Atticus because he was really well described by the author. I would definitely recommend it – it's a proper page-turner!
>
> (Red House catalogue, January 2013)

Encourage the pupils to look at the reviews written by children on the *Guardian*'s children's book pages at www.guardian.co.uk/books. They could submit reviews themselves or you could post their reviews on a school or class blog. Alternatively, you can put the finished reviews on display in the classroom or library or publish them in a class newsletter.

Activity sheet 12: planning a review of a novel

Use this sheet to help you to plan a book review.

Make notes on a separate piece of paper, before starting to write your review.

1 Write down the name of the author, the title of the book and the name of the publisher.
2 Find out about the author. Look at the cover and the blurb (the piece of writing about the book and its author). Visit the author's and the publisher's websites and make a note of any interesting facts about the author and the book that you could put in your review.
3 Look at the following types of book and decide which type of story it tells: mystery, adventure, ghost, science fiction, humorous, school, family, animal, sport, fantasy, crime, horror, war.
4 Is it one of a series of books? If so, what is the series called?
5 Think about what happens in the story. Make a list of the main events of the plot. (You could do this as a flow chart.)
6 Make a list of the main characters and what you like and dislike about them. Here's the start of such a list: Patricia: She's selfish and spoilt. She causes a lot of trouble. But she's brave.
7 What age-group do you think the story is for?
8 Do you think other people would enjoy this book? Note down what you liked and disliked about the book.
9 How do you rate the book on a five-star scale? (***** = excellent , * = poor)

Use your notes to help you to draft your review. Remember to use paragraphs. Here is the plan of a typical review:

Paragraph 1: Introduction – details of the title, the author and the type of book it is.

Paragraph 2: Who the main characters are and where the events take place.

Paragraph 3: The main details of the plot (but not including how the story ends!).

Paragraph 4: What you liked and disliked about the book, including what you found most interesting or exciting.

Paragraph 5: Conclusion – why you think other people would enjoy it or not enjoy it.

Curriculum opportunities

There are plenty of opportunities when studying a science, history or geography topic for writing reviews of non-fiction books.

Pupils can use the checklist on **Activity sheet 13: reviewing a non-fiction book** to help them to plan and draft their reviews.

Activity sheet 13: reviewing a non-fiction book

Use the checklist (below) to plan and draft a review of a non-fiction book.

1 Put the name of the author as well as the title of the book. Say if it is one of a series.

2 Look at the imprint page to see when the book was first published and put the date of publication. Ask yourself: Is it up-to-date?

3 Identify the subject of the book and in an introductory paragraph write one or two sentences saying what the book is about.

4 In the main part of the review summarise in paragraphs the most important things the author had to say about the subject.

5 What illustrations are there in the book? Are there any diagrams? Are the diagrams clear? Are there photographs or line drawings? Have they got captions? Are the captions clear?

6 Does the layout and design of the pages make it easy to follow the information? Are the headings clear? Is the information presented in the most logical way?

7 Include a paragraph commenting on the illustrations, layout and design of the book.

8 Is there an index? Is there a glossary? Is it easy to use the book to find out information on a particular feature of the book's subject?

9 Give your opinion of the book. Did the book answer your questions about the subject? What was the most interesting thing you learned about the subject? Was the information presented clearly? How does it compare with other books about the same subject?

Reviews of computer games

Put the review of Zoo Tycoon 2 (below) on the board and discuss how the writer explains the main points of the game in the first paragraph, goes into more detail and gives his view of it in the second paragraph, then gives his recommendation in the final paragraph.

Invite the pupils to write a review of a computer game using the review of Zoo Tycoon 2 as a model.

Zoo Tycoon 2

Zoo Tycoon 2 is a game in which players can create, manage and maintain their own zoo. Players have to research animals to put in the zoo, to manage the zoo's finances, to hire and monitor the staff and build exhibits. They can also step inside the zoo and experience it as a visitor.

Zoo Tycoon 2 is fun to play and at the same time teaches you all about zoos and the animals in them. Not only do you get to build your own zoo, but you have to run it and make sure that it is successful. For example, you have to set admission prices so that it will make a profit, but not so high that the prices don't attract enough visitors.

It is a game that is both entertaining and educational that I think 9–12 year olds would enjoy. I give it 5 stars.

Writing challenge

Pupils can imagine that they are a TV critic responsible for writing the 'Pick of the day' column in a newspaper or magazine. Encourage them to look at such columns in newspapers and listings magazines. Then invite them to think back to programmes that they have watched recently, to choose one that would have been their 'Pick of the day' and to write a review of it in no more than 50 words.

They could also choose a film they have watched recently, imagine that it is going to be on TV and write a 50-word recommendation of it as 'Film of the week'.

Part Three

Information writing

14   Biographies

A biography is an account of a person's life written by another person.

Explain that you can find short biographies of people in books such as *Who's Who*, on their internet websites and in encyclopaedias.

Such biographies try to contain as much information about the person as possible within a limited space.

Use **Activity sheet 14: a short biography**. Discuss how the information is presented so that as few words as possible are used. Then ask the children to suggest how they could cut 40 words from the article.

Activity sheet 14: a short biography

Korky Paul

Born in Zimbabwe in 1951. One of seven children. Christened Hamish Paul. Educated in South Africa at Estcourt High School and Durban School of Art. Worked for several years in advertising before becoming a full-time children's book illustrator. Best known for his illustrations of *Winnie the Witch* by Valerie Thomas, which won the Children's Book Award in 1985. *Winnie the Witch* has been translated into 10 languages and the series has sold millions worldwide. Has illustrated many other children's books, including poetry books such as *Dinosaur Poems* and *Dragon Poems*. He lives in Oxford, England and is married to the artist Susan Moxley. They have two grown-up children Zoe and Oska.

Notice how the information is presented so that as few words as possible are used. Pick out examples where the writer has written incomplete sentences, for example by leaving out the subject of the sentence.

Imagine you are the editor of a biographical dictionary in which this article is to be included and that to fit the space available it needs to be shortened by 40 words. On your own, decide which 40 words to cut, then compare your shortened versions in a group discussion.

Write an entry for a biographical dictionary about a member of your family, using no more than 100 words.

Use **Activity sheet 15: a class Who's Who**. Ask the children to work in pairs and to interview each other about their family, their interests, likes and dislikes, and ambitions, and to record their answers on the profile sheet. Explain that the person being interviewed need not stick to the truth. For the purpose of the exercise, they can be as inventive about their lives as they wish!

Using the information from the profile sheet, each person can then write a biographical article about their partner for a class who's who. You can either restrict them to writing a short biography of between 100 and 150 words or encourage them to draft a longer article, consisting of several paragraphs. The longer article could take the form of a feature article about the person for a newspaper or magazine.

Invite the children to interview an adult and to write a chapter of that person's life story. For example, they could interview an older person, such as a neighbour or grandparent, about a memorable period in their lives, for example about their experiences when they lived abroad or went travelling or their memories of their childhood or of a significant event in their lives. Encourage them either to take notes or to record the interview, so that they can check facts while they are writing.

Before they start their drafts, ask the children to think about how they are going to begin. Put these four opening sentences on the board and discuss which is the most interesting and why:

When she was eight, my gran had an accident.

Gran lived in the country when she was little and there was a wood nearby.

Gran was a bit of a tomboy as a child and she used to love climbing trees.

One day when she was eight, an event occurred that Gran remembers clearly.

When they have drafted the first paragraph, ask them to share it in a group. Get them to focus on the opening sentence. Is it dramatic? Does it capture the reader's attention? Could it be improved in any way? Whose is the best opening and why?

Curriculum opportunities

As part of an art project they could research a particular artist, such as Monet, and write an entry for a biographical dictionary similar to the one on Korky Paul.

Alternatively, they could focus on a musician as part of a music project.

They could also research and write entries for favourite authors and illustrators, for example Jacqueline Wilson, Michael Morpurgo, Quentin Blake, Roald Dahl.

As part of an RE topic, they could write a biography of an important religious figure, such as Mahatma Gandhi, Guru Nanak or Moses.

Activity sheet 15: a class Who's Who

PROFILE SHEET

Name

Date of birth

Birthplace

Current home address

Previous homes (if any)

Family details

Personal details (hair colour, height, etc.)

Schools attended

Hobbies and interests

Likes and dislikes (music, books, games, clothes, etc.)

Greatest achievements so far

Ambitions

15 Descriptions

Descriptions of people

Explain that a written description of a person will depend on the purpose of the description. If a police officer asks you for a description of someone who is suspected of committing a crime, you will concentrate on the person's appearance. On the other hand, if you are describing a character in a story, you will give details of the person's character as well as their appearance (see Chapter 25).

Ask them to imagine they saw someone being chased down the street and to write a description of their appearance and their clothes, as if they were writing a description for a police officer. Before they begin, brainstorm what details they would want to include, such as height, build, weight, colour of hair, skin or eyes, or any distinguishing features, such as freckles, glasses, tattoos, piercings, clothes, jewellery or shoes. Make a list on the board for them to refer to as they write.

Pupils can imagine that one of their friends is a smuggler, a pirate, a highwayman or a pickpocket and design a 'Wanted' poster describing their appearance and offering a reward for their capture.

Writing challenge

Invite the children to write a description of a person in the form of a poem which not only describes the person's appearance but also describes their character.

They could use 'Grandma' (below) as a model. Put the poem on the board and talk about how John Foster compares Grandma to various things: a colour, a piece of furniture, a sound, a place, a piece of clothing, a food or drink, an animal, a type of weather. They can then write their own eight-line poem, which consists of similar comparisons, about a person they know such as a family member, a teacher or a friend.

Grandma
Grandma is navy blue.
She is a comfy cushion.
Grandma is a soft whisper.
She is a path through a winter wood.
Grandma is a warm scarf.
She is a cup of tea by the fire.
Grandma is a sleeping cat.
She is autumn sunshine.

Descriptions of places

Explain that a written description of a place will depend on the purpose of the description. For example, the description of a town or village in a guide book or in an encyclopaedia will be written differently from a description of that town or village, which is being included in order to describe the setting for a story.

Put the following description of Abingdon-on-Thames on the board:

> Abingdon-on-Thames (population 36,000) is one of the oldest towns in England. Situated on the river Thames, nine kilometres from Oxford, it is the largest town in southern England with no railway service. For over 50 years, MG sports cars were made in Abingdon. In October, the town centre is closed for two days for the annual Ock Fair. On special occasions, such as royal weddings and jubilee celebrations, there is a bun throwing ceremony. Buns are thrown by local officials from the roof of a museum to a crowd which has gathered in the market square below.

Explain that this description comes from a guide book about Oxfordshire. It gives key facts about Abingdon's size and situation, then some interesting facts about the town in no particular order. Point out that space in a guide book is often limited, so entries have to be short. In this case, the description is fewer than 100 words.

Ask the pupils to write a description of the area of the city, the town or village in which they live, similar to the description of Abingdon. The description must be fewer than 100 words. Encourage them to brainstorm the facts they are going to include by drawing a spidergram on the board and asking for their suggestions.

Talk about how the description of Abingdon would be different if its purpose was not just to give facts about Abingdon, but to encourage people to visit Abingdon. You would try to make Abingdon seem an attractive place to visit in the way that the holiday advertisement for the Panorama Beach Hotel tries to make the hotel seem attractive (see Chapter 9). Invite them to rewrite their descriptions of the area in which they live in order to attract visitors to it.

Writing challenge

Write a description of a giant's castle without using the word 'the' in it.

Describing a room

Put this description of a room on the board:

> The room was dark, the only light coming from a small window, which overlooked the yard. The curtains were brown and looked in need of a wash. There was an armchair with a small table beside it in front of a gas fire. In the corner opposite was an old TV set. On one of the walls, there was a picture of a sailing ship in a storm. The carpet was threadbare and worn. It was a drab and dingy room, and not at all like the rooms in the house next door.

Explain that the description comes from a story. Ask the class what impression the writer gives of the room. Discuss how the writer creates this impression, first by the details that she includes and second by her choice of words.

Invite the children to write a description of a room, such as a room in a castle or a mansion, a room in a modern office block, a room in a police station or a dentist's, doctor's or hospital waiting room. Encourage them to start by thinking of the impression they want to give of the room. Put a list of adjectives on the board. They can include appropriate words from the list in their descriptions: ancient, antique, bright, cheerful, clean, cluttered, comfortable, cosy, dingy, drab, dreary, dull, dusty, gleaming, gloomy, grimy, homely, immaculate, luxurious, modern, old-fashioned, plain, spacious, sparkling, spotlesss, warm, welcoming.

Curriculum opportunities

During a history topic, they can look at pictures of rooms in particular buildings, for example in a Roman villa, a Norman castle or an Elizabethan manor house, and then write a description of one of the rooms.

When learning about Shakespeare they can research what the Globe Theatre looked like, imagine they attended a play and write a description of the theatre.

16   Directions

Directions are instructions of how to get from one place to another.

Put the example below on the board and discuss the features of a good set of directions. Point out how they are arranged clearly step by step and that each step consists of a single sentence. Draw attention to the use of 'bossy' verbs, the mention of the distances involved and the use of street names and landmarks, such as the newsagent's and the church.

How to get to school from my house:

Turn right outside my house and walk about 50 yards to the end of Coleridge Road.

Turn left at the T-junction and cross the road at the traffic lights.

Go another 20 yards and turn right at the newsagent's into Bryants Close.

Follow the road past the row of shops and the Catholic church.

You will see the entrance to the school on your left.

Ask the children to write directions about how to walk to the school from somewhere which is about a mile from the school, such as their home, the local supermarket, a playground, a church or another landmark.

When they have finished, ask them to form groups and to share their directions with the rest of the group. Discuss whose are the easiest to follow and why.

Writing challenge

Write a set of directions explaining how to get from your home to the nearest post office without using the letter 'g'.

Invite individuals to imagine they are part of a pirate crew. Write the directions explaining where you have buried the treasure on a desert island. You could begin the directions with the following sentence: 'Anchor in Deadman's Cove and row ashore.'

Pupils can imagine they are playing a computer game, which involves finding a crystal inside a castle. They meet a wizard who gives them a parchment on which are written directions explaining how to get to the room where the crystal is. Ask them to write the directions given on the parchment.

Curriculum opportunities

There are opportunities for writing directions when you are teaching map reading skills. Encourage the pupils in pairs to work out and write directions for getting from one landmark to another.

17 Explanations

Explanations provide information about how to do something, how something works or why something happens or happened in the past.

Writing explanations

Explain that there are two types of explanations depending on their purpose:

1 Explanations which focus on 'how'. These include directions of how to get somewhere (see Chapter 16), instructions on how to do something or how to make something (see Chapter 19) and recipes of how to make foods (see Chapter 22).

   There are also explanations of how things work, such as how the brakes on a bicycle work or how a computer works, and explanations of processes, such as the life cycle of a butterfly or how a volcano is formed.
2 Explanations which focus on 'why'. Examples are: Why do certain objects float while others sink? Why is the rainforest disappearing? Why did the Egyptians build pyramids? Why are tigers an endangered species?

Explaining how something works

Use **Activity sheet 16: explanations – how something works**. Talk about the features of this type of explanation. There is an introduction consisting of one or two sentences identifying what is to be explained. The information is then presented in a logical order using time connectives, such as *first*, *then* and *when*. Point out that the present tense is used throughout. Then ask the children to write their own explanations of how something works.

   Discuss which items they found easiest to explain and which were the hardest. Ask them to focus on one of the harder ones and to draft an explanation of what it is, what it is used for and how it works.

Activity sheet 16: explanations – how something works

This explanation is from a book on railways.

How a steam locomotive works

An engine that is powered by steam is called a steam locomotive. This is how a steam locomotive works.

A steam locomotive has a boiler full of water. First, steam is made by heating the water. There is a coal fire in what is known as the firebox. A person known as the fireman stands beside the driver and shovels coal into the engine's firebox. As the fire gets hot, the heat from the fire makes the water boil.

Steam from the boiler then goes along a steam-pipe to the engine's cylinders. Here the pressure of the steam drives pistons up and down inside the cylinders. The pistons are joined by rods to the driving wheels. So when the pistons go up and down, they move the rods and the wheels turn.

In pairs take it in turns to choose an item from the list below and to explain to their partner what it is, what it is used for and how it works: screwdriver, corkscrew, needle, stapler, toaster, electric kettle, torch, shoe horn, vice, compass.

Explaining why something happens

Pupils are often asked to write explanations of why something happens as part of a science topic.

Put the explanation of why water freezes from **Activity sheet 17: explanations – explaining why** on the board. Point out the features of this type of explanation. The information is presented in a logical order, using connectives such as *when*, *as* and *so*. The present tense is used, and the verbs are mostly active, though it ends with a passive *ice is formed*.

Ask the pupils to write a similar explanation of why water boils. Alternatively, they could write an explanation of a natural phenomenon, such as why tsunamis occur.

Explaining why something happened

This type of explanation is used when writing about historical events, such as why the Vikings invaded Britain (see Activity sheet 17).

Put the explanation on the board. Point out that, in this instance, the past tense is used. Invite the pupils to write a similar explanation of a historical event, such as why children were evacuated from London during the Second World War.

Activity sheet 17: explanations – explaining why

Study the explanation of why water freezes, then write an explanation of why water boils.

Why water freezes

Water consists of tiny particles called molecules. When water loses heat as it gets colder, these molecules move more slowly. Eventually, when the temperature reaches 0 centigrade, they stick together. The water changes from a liquid into a solid and ice is formed.

Study the explanation of why the Vikings invaded Britain, then write a similar explanation of a historical event.

Why the Vikings invaded Britain

There are two main reasons why the Vikings invaded Britain.

The first invaders were bands of robbers. They raided the monasteries and stole silver, gold and jewels. Then they went back home to Scandinavia.

Later, the Vikings came to Britain to stay. They settled in Britain and became farmers and traders. They came in search of farmland, because the land in Norway was too hilly, the land in Sweden was covered in forests and in Denmark the soil was very sandy.

Assessing explanations

Use **Activity sheet 18: comparing paragraphs**. The children have to work in groups comparing the three paragraphs, discussing which is the best and giving their reasons, before awarding marks out of ten for each paragraph. They can then assess each other's drafts of why a historical event happened (see **Activity sheet 17: explanations – explaining why**) before redrafting them.

Activity sheet 18: comparing paragraphs

These children were asked to write a paragraph explaining why children were evacuated during the Second World War. In groups, discuss which is the best paragraph and why and decide how many marks out of ten you would give each paragraph.

Lots of children were evacuated during the Second World War. They had labels put round their necks and were taken to the country in trains. They were met at the station and told which family they were going to live with. They were evacuated because of the bombing. Some of the adults treated the children cruelly and I wouldn't have liked to be an evacuee.

(Parveen)

Children were evacuated during the Second World War because of the dangers of staying in the cities. Many people were killed and lost their homes when the Germans bombed cities, such as London. So London children were sent to live with other families in places where it was safer. The Germans also bombed cities, such as Coventry and Oxford, where there were factories. The children went to stay in the country, for example in Wales, where there was less chance of them being bombed.

(Sadie)

Children were sent away from home during the Second World War. They went because the German aircraft were attacking London. The RAF fought the German planes in the Battle of Britain in order to stop the Germans dropping bombs. The children who were evacuated were called evacuees. Many evacuees were unhappy because they were separated from their families.

(Matthew)

Writing tip: writing paragraphs

Remind them what a paragraph is – a group of sentences, all of which are about the same idea or subject.

Put up the paragraph about 'Holidaying in Spain' (below) on the board and explain how they can use the five-step or 1–2–3–4–5 method of building up a paragraph.

Holidaying in Spain

There are three reasons why Spain is a good place to go on holiday. First, there is the climate, which means that it is hotter in Spain in the summer than it is in Britain. Second, Spain has some of the best beaches in Europe. Finally, there are lots of good hotels and apartments, which are quite cheap. So Spain is a very popular holiday destination.

Talk about how the paragraph starts with a topic sentence (1), stating the idea or subject of the paragraph. Then, there are three sentences (2, 3, 4), which give details, facts and examples to support the main subject or idea. There is a final sentence (5) restating the main idea or subject.

Put a page from an information book about the topic you are studying on the board. Ask the pupils how many paragraphs there are on the page and discuss how we know where a new paragraph starts.

Explain that the first sentence of a new paragraph always starts on a new line and that there is always a space between the first word of a new paragraph and the margin of the page. Often, there is also a blank line, known as a line space, between paragraphs.

Curriculum opportunities

There are many opportunities for writing explanations in science lessons, for example an explanation of why some objects float, while others sink. Other examples include explanations of life cycles, such as the life cycles of butterflies and frogs, and of how parts of the body work, such as the eye or the heart.

There are similar opportunities during geography topics. For example, they can write explanations of what happens when a volcano erupts or what causes an earthquake.

You can also write explanations as part of a music project. Put the entry for the trumpet (below) on the board. Talk about the information it gives. Invite groups to write similar entries about other musical instruments and to produce a booklet – an encyclopaedia of musical instruments.

As part of a project on Ancient Egypt, pupils can write an explanation of how the pyramids were built or why the River Nile was so important in Ancient Egypt.

How a trumpet works

The trumpet is a brass instrument. You make sounds by blowing into a mouthpiece with your lips pressed together. There are valves which you press with your fingers to make different notes. The valves change the length of tubing that the air goes through so they change the notes you make.

18 Glossaries

A glossary is an alphabetical list of terms connected with a particular subject together with an explanation of their meanings.

Explain what a glossary is and how a glossary is often found at the back of an information text. Find an information book, show the class an example of a glossary and read out one or two examples of the definitions of the terms it includes.

Write some examples from a glossary on the board. For example, put up some terms from a glossary in a book about smuggling:

cask a barrel containing spirits, such as brandy

contraband smuggled goods on which tax has not been paid

customs duty tax on goods being imported or exported

free-traders smugglers

run a smuggling operation

sowing the crop hiding contraband offshore under the sea to be collected or 'reaped' later

stinkibus casks of spirits which have gone bad through being too long in the sea

Ask the pupils in pairs to prepare a glossary of terms about school, which could be given to a space visitor from another planet to explain the everyday terms used in school. Either ask the children to make their own lists of terms or brainstorm a list with the class and put it on the board, explaining that they will need to include all the terms we use such as: class, pupil, teacher, term, lesson, books, assembly, caretaker, headteacher, playground. Encourage them to use dictionaries to help them with their definitions.

Give out copies of **Activity sheet 19: a pirate glossary** for the pupils to complete.

Curriculum opportunities

When you are studying a topic, encourage the pupils to compile glossaries of terms that are specific to that topic. For example, when you are studying a historical topic, such as the Romans or the Egyptians, encourage the class to build up a glossary. You can put the glossary on the computer, encourage individuals to add terms to it and then print out a copy to put on the classroom wall.

Activity sheet 19: a pirate glossary

Write in the meaning of each term. Use a dictionary or an encyclopaedia to help you.

buccaneer

Caribbean

cat-o'-nine tails

cutlass

desert island

doubloon

galleon

grappling iron

jolly roger

maroon

mutiny

pieces of eight

pirate

pistol

press gang

scurvy

Spanish main

walk the plank

19 Instructions

Instructions explain how something is done, for example by setting out the rules of a game or telling you the steps you need to take in order to make something, as in a recipe (see Chapter 22).

Introduce the topic by demonstrating how to make something simple, such as a bookmark, a paper aeroplane or a greetings card. Then ask the pupils to write a set of instructions explaining how to make whatever it is that you made.

Assessing instructions

Get the pupils to compare their instructions and discuss whose instructions are the clearest and why. Explain that the clearest instructions have the following features:

- a clear and precise title stating what the end result will be;
- a list of the materials needed and any tools or equipment required;
- a series of numbered points giving a step-by-step list of what needs to be done, arranged in the order in which each action is to be done;
- each step begins with a 'bossy verb' and states clearly and simply what needs to be done;
- pictures and/or diagrams used as necessary to make the explanation clearer.

Ask the children which card games they know and invite pupils in groups to teach each other how to play card games such as Beggar My Neighbour. Then invite them to write a set of instructions explaining how to play one of the games they have been playing.

Talk about the importance of giving instructions in the right order. Divide the class into groups and give out **Activity sheet 20: the dictionary game**, which presents a set of rules in a wrong order. Pupils have to work out the correct order and try to play the game. They then have to discuss how clear the rules are and suggest how they might be altered in order to make them clearer.

Activity sheet 20: the dictionary game

The instructions for this game are in the wrong order. Decide what is the correct order, then try to play the game. Afterwards, discuss how clear the instructions are. Suggest how you could alter them in order to make them clearer.

The dictionary game
For two or more players
Playing time 20–40 minutes
You will need a dictionary, pencils, paper.

1   When five minutes are up, the players take it in turns to read out words with their three definitions.
2   The game continues until all the words have been read out; the player with the highest number of points is the winner.
3   You will probably need three words and definitions for each player (or team).
4   Give each player his list of words and definitions.
5   Then, write out each word clearly on a large sheet of paper, ready to stick on the wall.
6   After a couple of minutes, all the pieces of paper are collected up, the true definition is read out and everybody who guessed correctly is given a point.
7   Go through the dictionary picking out a number of unusual words.
8   Stick the word that is being read out up on the wall, so that everybody can see how it is spelt.
9   They then have five minutes to make up two false definitions for each word on their lists, making sure that none of the other players can see what they are doing.
10 Write the players' words with their definitions on a piece of paper to give to them, making a note for yourself of which player has which words.
11 As soon as all three definitions have been read out, all the other players quietly decide which definition each of them thinks is the true definition and write it down on a piece of paper.
12 They should write all three definitions (one true and two false) on another sheet of paper, so that there is no way that the opposition can see which definition is the true one.

Curriculum opportunities

During a topic on myths and legends, the pupils can make finger puppets or face masks of the people and creatures involved in particular stories. Having made the puppets or masks they can write a set of instructions explaining how to make them.

As part of a technology project in which they are designing and making a board game, pupils can be asked not only to write a set of rules for the game, but also a set of instructions to explain how to make the board game.

Pupils can read the story *George's Marvellous Medicine* by Roald Dahl. They can then write a set of instructions explaining how to make the medicine. George actually makes four different medicines. Abler writers could write the instructions for all four and then compare them to see why they had different effects.

In an IT lesson, pupils can write a set of instructions explaining how to perform a particular task on a computer, for example how to carry out a search using a search engine.

20 Invitations

A written invitation asks someone if they would like to attend an event, such as a party.

Explain that any invitation needs to contain certain key pieces of information. Ask the pupils to suggest what key information you would need to include if you were inviting someone to a birthday party which consists of a trip to the cinema to see a film, followed by tea at McDonald's. Draw up a checklist on the board of all the information you would need to put in the invitation.

The checklist should include:

- the name of the person holding the party;
- the reason for the party;
- what form the party will take;
- what date the party is to be held;
- where and when to meet for the party;
- what food will be provided;
- where and when the party will end;
- where a reply should be sent;
- the date by which a reply needs to be sent.

Ask the children to design and make an invitation to a pirate party for someone's birthday. They could write the invitation on a treasure map or a treasure chest and use pirate language; for example, it could begin: 'Ahoy, there, you scurvy landlubber!'

Alternatively, they could design an invitation to a football party. This could be written on a football or a football pitch, or it could take the form of a ticket to a football match. For example, the ticket would include the time of the kick-off, details of the venue and who to contact to confirm their attendance.

They can refer to the checklist to make sure they include all the relevant information.

Writing challenge

Ask the children to imagine they receive an invitation to a sleepover at Dracula's Castle, at the Mad Magician's Mansion or in the Cyclops' Cavern, or to spend a free night at the Hallowe'en Hotel, at the Ghastly Grange Country Club or the Troll's Tavern. They can write and design one or more of the invitations.

21 Newspaper reports

Explain that newspapers contain several different kinds of reports and articles. These range from factual reports of events to articles and editorials expressing opinions.

Writing newspaper reports

Prepare for the topic by collecting copies of newspapers. Use them to explain the difference between a newspaper report and a newspaper article. Point out that reports give facts about news stories, while articles often contain opinions as well as facts. Often, the front half of a newspaper concentrates on reports, while the second half contains a mixture of articles, puzzles, listings, letters and reviews.

Either study one or more of the news reports from the newspapers you have collected or put this report on the board.

> Pupils at Hightown Primary School in Westshire raised £234 from a non-uniform day last week. The money is being sent to help the Disasters Relief Organisation set up camps for the victims of the earthquake in Pakistan. 'It was the children's own idea,' said headteacher Sonia Blanks. 'They suggested it after seeing pictures of homeless families on TV.'

Write 'WHO? WHAT? WHEN? WHERE? WHY?' on the board. Explain that the writer of a newspaper report sets out to tell the reader the answer to these five questions (the 'Five Ws'). Discuss how the journalist tries to answer as many of these questions as possible in the first sentence, then gives more details in the rest of the story.

Writing tip: using direct and indirect speech

Explain that in newspaper reports we often include something a person has said. In the report on Hightown's non-uniform day, the reporter quotes what the headteacher actually said. Point out that this is called direct speech and the words she actually spoke are put inside speech marks.

Write on the board what the reporter would have written if he had used indirect speech: 'The headteacher said that it was the children who had suggested the idea after seeing pictures of homeless families on TV.' Explain the difference between indirect and direct speech and stress that we do not use speech marks in indirect speech.

Reinforce their understanding by drawing two columns on the board labelled 'Direct speech' and 'Indirect speech', and listing some examples:

Direct speech	**Indirect speech**
Jane said, 'It was an accident.'	Jane said that it was an accident.
'It was definitely a penalty,' the manager said.	The manager said that it was definitely a penalty.

Ask the children to suggest further examples.

Ask the pupils in groups of four to work together to produce a class news-sheet consisting of four items of news about events that have taken place at school during the past month. Each of them should write one of the reports. Encourage them to show each other their draft reports and to check that they have included answers to the 'Five Ws'. They can then put their reports on the computer and design and produce their news-sheets. You can compare their news-sheets in a class discussion, deciding which is the best and why.

Use **Activity sheet 21: nursery rhyme news reports** to get the pupils to write news reports of their own based on a nursery rhyme.

The Rhymes Times

Two injured in track tumble

Two children are being treated in hospital for injuries they received yesterday when they were coming down Windy Hill. Jack Lemon, aged 11, of 99 Nursery Close, Storyville, and his neighbour, Jill Orange, aged 10, of 113 Nursery Close, had gone up Windy Hill to collect water from the pump. As they were coming down the track, Jack tripped on a stone and lost his balance.

Jill said, 'He let go of the bucket which we were carrying together. The water went everywhere and I came tumbling after him.'

They were found lying in a heap by Little Bo-Peep, who was searching for her lost sheep. She called an ambulance and they were taken to King Cole hospital. An X-ray revealed that Jack has a broken crown. He has been kept in for observation.

A local resident, Mary Contrary, of Cockleshell Gardens, said: 'The track down Windy Hill is in urgent need of repair. There are lots of loose stones and potholes. It is particularly dangerous if you are carrying water down from the pump.'

Discuss how the article is based on the nursery rhyme about Jack and Jill. Then write an article of your own based on a nursery rhyme. You could use one of the following as the headline for your article:

EXCITED COW IN MOON JUMP

BIRD PECKS OFF MAID'S NOSE IN PALACE GARDEN

COCK ROBIN MURDER – SPARROW CONFESSES

FARMER'S WIFE GUILTY OF CRUELTY TO MICE

The 'Five Ws' game

Recap the 'Five Ws' by playing the Who? What? When? Where? Why? game. Explain that this is a game for five players and hand out pieces of paper.

1   Each person writes 'WHO?' on the paper and then adds a name and description of a character. It can be a character from a myth or fairy tale, or a fictional character they have invented such as Ben D. Man, a contortionist, Dr Digger, an archaeologist, or Mr Deadbody, a teacher. If appropriate, encourage them to include the person's age and address.
2   They then fold the paper so that what they have written cannot be seen and pass it to the person on their right. This person writes 'WHAT?' on the paper and makes up what has happened to the person. For example, the person was arrested, fell down a mineshaft, was kidnapped by aliens, or saw a ghost. Encourage them to be imaginative.
3   This person folds the paper so that what they have written cannot be seen and passes it on.
4   The next person writes 'WHEN?' and gives a time the event occurred. Explain that they can put either real times, such as yesterday afternoon or ridiculous times such as 5,000 years ago or next Tuesday.
5   The paper is folded again and passed on to the next person who writes 'WHERE?' and describes where the event happened. Again, encourage them to be imaginative, for example at the top of the Eiffel Tower or at the South Pole. They then fold the paper and pass it on.
6   The last person writes 'WHY?' and gives an explanation as to why the event occurred. This person needs to think of an event, such as an accident, a discovery or a disaster, and a reason for it, such as because they were looking for their spectacles or not doing their homework. Once again, encourage them to be imaginative.

When all five people have written on the paper, they can look at the ridiculous newspaper stories they have created. Get them to share the funniest ones with the rest of the class.

Headline writing

Explain that the purpose of a headline is to summarise what a story is about and that a good headline usually consists of between five and ten words.

Put these examples of headlines on the board and ask pairs to decide which of the headlines is the best and why, then share their views in a class discussion:

1   'Animal has to be rescued from tree'; 'Cat gets stuck up tree'; 'Fire brigade to the rescue'; 'Fireman rescues stranded cat'
2   'Local girl triumphs'; 'Local girl wins audition for talent show'; 'Teenage dancer in talent show triumph'; 'Tina to dance on TV'
3   'Injured circus performer in hospital'; 'Circus show halted by accident'; 'Trapeze artist badly hurt in fall'; 'Horror as trapeze artist loses her grip'

Use **Activity sheet 22: writing headlines**. Ask the pupils to write headlines for the four reports, then compare them, discussing whose is the best and why.

Activity sheet 22: writing headlines

The aim of a headline is to summarise what a newspaper report is about and to attract the interest of the readers, so that they will go on to read the story.

Read these newspaper stories and write a headline for each one. Then compare your headlines with other people's headlines and decide whose works best and why.

Charlie Smithers, aged 9, was walking his dog Snuffles across the moor yesterday, when it fell down a hole which suddenly appeared beside the path. The dog had fallen down one of the old mineshafts that are scattered across the moor. He was rescued by a local potholer, Jim Briggs, who was passing.

Brillington Primary School's Under 11s continued their unbeaten run with a 6–0 victory over local rivals St Swithun's. Captain Jamie Lee scored a hat-trick and Wesley Green, Tom Knight and Grant Poulter scored a goal each. Six of the Brillington team have been selected to play for the County Under 11s.

St Jasper's Primary School will remain closed for the rest of this week, as staff deal with the damage caused by the flood when the river Wendrush broke its banks. Nearly a month's rain fell in twenty-four hours last Tuesday. Caretaker Richard Mullins, who lives on the premises, had to be evacuated from his bungalow.

Villagers from Winkersbury staged a protest at the site where a new incinerator is to be built next year. The landfill site at Lower Winkersbury is due to be closed and councillors say that the new incinerator is necessary to deal with the growing amount of waste produced in the area. Local residents say the incinerator will be an eyesore and a blot on the countryside.

Wacky headlines

Play the 'Wacky headlines' game. This is a game for five players which shows how four-word headlines can be created. You need to have slips of paper on which single words can be written and four envelopes in which to put the slips of paper.

First, each person writes three different adjectives on three slips of paper. Encourage them to think of powerful adjectives, such as gigantic, courageous and cunning, as well as well-used ones, such as good and nice. The slips of paper then go into envelope 1.

Next, each person writes the names of three people or animals on three slips of paper. They can be real or imaginary – a pirate, a plumber, an alligator or a unicorn. The slips of paper are put in envelope 2.

Next, each person writes three verbs, which describe actions, on three slips of paper. The verbs should be in the present tense, for example cooks, strikes, embraces. The slips of paper are then put in envelope 3.

Finally, each person writes three nouns on three slips of paper, for example hens, books, clocks, trousers. The slips of paper are put in envelope 4.

The players take it in turns to draw slips from the envelopes to make wacky headlines, for example 'Gigantic frog crushes clocks', 'Courageous unicorn boils trousers'.

Curriculum opportunities

When you are studying a history topic, such as the Romans or the Second World War, there is the opportunity to ask the pupils to show their knowledge of a particular event by writing a newspaper report. For example, they could write a newspaper report about the bombing of London during the Blitz.

As part of a geography project, they could write a newspaper report of a natural disaster, such as a volcanic eruption (e.g. the Mount St Helens eruption in 1980), an earthquake (e.g. the San Francisco earthquake in 1906) or a flood (e.g. the Indian Ocean tsunami in 2004).

22   Recipes

A recipe is a list of ingredients and instructions explaining how to make something, usually a type of food.

Explain what a recipe is and put up an example on the board. Talk about how the recipe begins with a statement which says what is to be made. This is followed by a list of the ingredients, including the quantity of each ingredient, then step-by-step instructions explaining how the particular food is made.

Point out how each of the instructions begins with a verb which tells you what needs to be done.

Before they write their own recipes, ask the pupils to think of as many verbs as they can which describe what you do when cooking or preparing food, such as peel, boil, fry. Build up a list on the board. Then hand out **Activity sheet 23: cooking verbs** for the pupils to complete. Encourage them to compare their definitions of the cookery words with the definitions given in a dictionary.

Use **Activity sheet 24: gruesome grub** and invite the pupils to write a recipe for a disgusting dish. They can put their recipes on the computer and print them out in a Gruesome Grub Cookery Book.

Activity sheet 23: cooking verbs

In the space provided, give the meaning of each of these cooking verbs:

bake

beat

boil

chop

crush

fry

grate

mince

mix

peel

pour

roast

simmer

slice

stir

strain

whisk

Activity sheet 24: gruesome grub

Here is a recipe from the book describing how to make a slug sandwich:

How to make a slug sandwich

Ingredients:

Two slices of mouldy bread

A pat of rancid butter

Six squashed slugs

A teaspoonful of slime

Three or four nettle leaves

Instructions:

1 Cut two slices of bread from a mouldy loaf.
2 Spread one side of each slice with rancid butter.
3 Place the slugs on the buttered side of one of the slices.
4 Put the nettle leaves on top of the slugs.
5 Sprinkle a teaspoonful of slime over the slugs.
6 Place the buttered side of the other slice of bread on top of the slugs and nettle leaves.
7 Cut the two slices of bread into four and serve with a garnish of thistles.

Write a recipe for a disgusting dish such as maggot pie, crunchy cockroaches in compost or bats' wing soup.

Make a book of recipes for imaginary desserts such as Pirate's Pudding, Jack Horner's Pie, Mermaid's Delight, Queen of Hearts Tarts, Mother Hubbard's Magic Muffins or Simple Simon's Surprise.

© 2014, *Let's Write*, John Foster, Routledge

Writing challenge

Ask the children to write a recipe for a witch's stew without using the letter 'a'.

Curriculum opportunities

As part of a cookery project, the children can write recipes for a favourite dish, which they can then illustrate. They can design and print a class recipe book, which they can sell to parents at an event such as a Christmas fair.

23 Reports (non-chronological reports)

Reports which are written in order to describe the way things are or the way things used to be are known as non-chronological reports.

Explain the purpose of non-chronological reports and discuss how they occur, for example in science books in order to describe different types of animals or plants, or in geography books to describe different places or features and in history books to describe the different lives people led.

Because they describe the way things are or used to be rather than recounting a series of events in the order they occurred, they are called non-chronological reports.

Writing a report about an animal

Talk about how non-chronological reports have the same structure whatever the topic. Make copies of **Activity sheet 25: writing a report** for the pupils to study. It consists of a report that Suzy wrote about grey squirrels.

Point out that her report follows the three-point paragraph plan that all reports have:

1 an introduction;
2 separate paragraphs on particular features;
3 a conclusion.

Explain that the introduction is a clear statement of the topic: the grey squirrel.

The paragraphs have a logical order but are not in time order and each paragraph focuses on one feature of the topic – what it looks like, what it eats, what it does.

There is a conclusion consisting of a statement that rounds off the topic in some way – some people regard the grey squirrel as a pest.

Invite the children to write a similar report about a bird or animal that lives in Britain so that you can produce a class booklet of British birds and animals. Encourage them to research the topic in books and on the internet, make notes on what they find out, and then make a plan before drafting their reports.

Activity sheet 25: writing a report

The grey squirrel

The grey squirrel is a small mammal which lives in woodlands, parks and gardens.

There are about 2 million grey squirrels in Britain.

Squirrels have long, bushy tails and large eyes. Consequently, they have good eyesight.

They have strong, sharp claws which help them to climb trees and are very agile. Did you know they can jump six metres?

Squirrels are mainly herbivores. They eat leaves, nuts and seeds. But they sometimes eat small insects and take the eggs from birds' nests.

They build nests called dreys high up in trees. However, they spend most of the time foraging for food on the ground.

The grey squirrel was introduced into England from North America. As a result there has been a decline in the number of red squirrels. So some people regard the grey squirrel as a pest.

(Suzy)

© 2014, *Let's Write*, John Foster, Routledge

Make copies of **Activity sheet 26: assessing reports** and **Activity sheet 27: comparing reports**. Ask groups to compare the two reports on the lives of Victorian children. Discuss the structure, language and content of each report. Who has written the better report? Share their views in a whole-class discussion.

Activity sheet 26: assessing reports

Use this checklist to assess and compare reports.

The structure:

1 Is the title clear? Is there a clear introduction which explains what is being described?
2 Could the opening be written more clearly?
3 Are there separate paragraphs used to describe different features?
4 Does each paragraph deal with one feature? Are there any paragraphs that need to be divided up into two separate paragraphs?
5 Are the paragraphs arranged in a logical order? Would it improve the structure of the report to change the order of the paragraphs?
6 Are headings used? Would it be helpful to add headings?
7 Is there a conclusion? Is it effective? Has the writer fallen into the trap of simply repeating what has already been stated? Could it be improved and, if so, how?

The language:

1 Is the report written in a formal style, avoiding the use of slang?
2 Is the writing impersonal? Does the writer make the mistake of including his opinions rather than just giving the facts?
3 Is the report written in the appropriate tense (usually the present tense, except for historical reports)?
4 Has the writer included technical vocabulary and clearly explained what the technical terms mean?
5 Does the writer make good use of connectives? Are there any places where a sentence could be improved by the use of a connective?

The content:

1 Is there something about the subject that you think the report should have contained but doesn't?
2 Does the report include examples? Would it have been useful to include more examples?
3 Are diagrams included? Are any diagrams clearly captioned and labelled? Would it have helped to include a diagram?
4 Is the report interesting? Could it have been more interesting? How could it have been made more interesting?

Activity sheet 27: comparing reports

Victorian children's lives

Children in Victorian times led very different lives from ours.

Education

For a start, many children did not go to school. There were schools for the rich, such as dame schools and public schools. But the majority of children had no education. Education for all children was not introduced until towards the end of Queen Victoria's reign.

Work

Many children had to go to work, because their families were so poor. They worked in mines and in factories.

Because they were small, they were made to crawl under machines and to work as chimney sweeps. The work was dangerous and many of them were injured and some were killed. They weren't paid very much either.

Homes

Rich people lived in huge houses, but the majority of people lived in slums. There was no sanitation and people had to share toilets and fetch water from standpipes. They had baths in tin baths and had to share the bathwater. Diseases were common and many children died before the age of five.

Life for Victorian children was much harder than life is for us.

(Jasmeen)

Victorian children

Victorian children lived 200 years ago during the reign of Queen Victoria.

Schools

A lot of children did not go to school, because there were no schools for them to go to. So a lot of them could not read or write.

They went to work down mines, or in factories. Some of them even climbed up chimneys.

There was a man called Dr Barnardo and he set up a school and homes for orphans and street children.

Slums

Many children lived in slums. They did not have toilets in their houses. They had to share a toilet with several other families. They were very poor and some of them did not even have shoes.

People had lots of children, but a lot of children died before the age of 5.

Life wasn't much fun for Victorian children.

(Laura)

In groups, compare these two reports. Discuss who has written the better report and list the reasons why you think it is a better report.

© 2014, *Let's Write*, John Foster, Routledge

Curriculum opportunities

Pupils can research what life was like for children growing up in medieval times, then write a report about growing up in medieval England.

24 Summaries

A summary is a shortened account containing the main points of a longer piece of writing, such as a page of a book or an article in a magazine.

Explain that the object of a summary is to pick out the main points of the article or passage you are summarising. Hand out copies of **Activity sheet 28: making a summary**. Explain that in order to make a summary they need to read the passage closely, identifying what the topic is, what each paragraph is about and any key words that are introduced. Ask them either individually or in pairs to use three different coloured highlighter pens and to use one colour to highlight the topic of the passage, another colour to highlight the topic sentences in each paragraph and a third colour to highlight the key words that are introduced. When they have finished, put a copy of the activity sheet on the board and discuss which sentences and key words they have highlighted.

Then invite them to write a summary of the passage.

Assessing summaries

They can then compare their summaries in groups and decide which of their summaries they think is the best. You can then discuss with them what are the features of a good summary, using either Stuart's summary (below) or one of their summaries as an example.

> There were two groups of dinosaurs: lizard-hipped and bird-hipped. Some lizard-hipped dinosaurs, called theropods, were carnivorous. Others called sauropods were herbivorous. The sauropods may have been amphibious.
>
> (Stuart)

Explain that a good summary:

is much shorter than the original passage;

includes all the main points;

is in your own words and is not just a copy of the original.

Activity sheet 28: making a summary

Types of dinosaurs

Scientists divide dinosaurs into two main groups. The difference between the two kinds is the shape of their hip bones. Some dinosaurs had hip bones that were shaped like those of a lizard. They are known as the lizard-hipped dinosaurs. In other dinosaurs, the bones were arranged differently. Their hip bones look rather like those of a bird, so they are known as the bird-hipped dinosaurs.

There were two different groups of lizard-hipped dinosaurs. One group were meat-eaters. Animals which eat meat are said to be carnivorous. The carnivorous dinosaurs with lizard-hips are known as theropods.

The other group of lizard-hipped dinosaurs were mainly plant-eaters. Animals which eat only plants are said to be herbivorous. The herbivorous dinosaurs are known as sauropods.

Some scientists think that these dinosaurs lived in water most of the time. Other scientists think that they went into the water only now and then. Animals that can live in water and on land are said to be amphibious. We do not know for certain that the sauropods were amphibious.

Use three different coloured highlighters. Highlight the topic of the passage in one colour, for example red. Then highlight the topic sentence of each paragraph in another colour, for example yellow. Use a third colour to highlight key words, for example green. Write a summary of the passage.

Curriculum opportunities

There are many opportunities when pupils are researching a topic in science, history or geography for the pupils to write a summary. For example, they can write a summary of the information they find in an encyclopaedia or on a website about a particular subject, such as Norman castles.

Part Four

Creative writing

25   Stories

Ask individuals to make a list of different types of story. Then hold a class discussion and put a list of different types of story on the board. Point out that stories can be categorised by their general type – adventure, ghost, mystery, science fiction, thriller – or by their theme – family, school, sport, space. Before you start to write a story, you need to think about what type of story you are going to write, the purpose of the story and the point of view from which the story is going to be written.

The purpose of the story

Discuss how it can be difficult to come up with an idea for your story. Explain that one way of doing so is to start with a problem; for example the problem might be that someone is under suspicion and is being falsely accused of doing something, or the problem might be that someone is trapped somewhere. Once you have decided on the problem, ask yourself: Who has the problem? What are they going to do about it? What difficulties do they encounter in trying to solve the problem?

Suggest that asking the question 'What if ...?' is another way of getting an idea. There are innumerable possibilities, such as: What if I was captured by aliens? What if I were to be invisible? What if I woke up to find myself in a different family in a different century? What if a wizard turned me into an animal? What if I found a baby dragon?

Explain that once you have the idea for a story, you need to think about the purpose of the story. Is the aim of the story to show how the characters react in a certain situation or how they manage to solve a particular problem? Does the story have a message or moral?

Either help them to come up with an idea by themselves or ask them to write a particular type of story.

Planning a story 1: the plot

Explain that when you have thought of an idea for a story, the next step is to make a plot. The plot of a story is the outline of events that take place in the story. Explain that you can make the plan of a plot by drawing a storyboard or a flow chart.

Writing tip: making a plot

Explain that a good plot has four key features:

1 an interesting beginning that engages the reader and grabs his attention;
2 a conflict or a problem that needs to be resolved;
3 a climax;
4 a resolution of the conflict or problem.

Put **Activity sheet 29: a ghost story** on the board. Explain how the plot of a story can be shown in a flow chart giving the series of events. Invite the children in groups to think up the plot of a ghost story and to present it in the form of a flow chart. They can then individually write a version of the story. They can compare their versions and discuss whose version is the best and why.

Activity sheet 29: a ghost story

Every story has a plot. The plot is the outline of the series of events that happen in the story. Often you can sum up the plot in a few sentences, or you can show it in the form of a flow chart. This flow chart shows the plot of a ghost story called 'Abigail and Jack'.

Abigail, a rich farmer's daughter,
falls in love with Jack, a farm labourer.

They meet in secret in the churchyard and want to marry.

Abigail's father finds out.
He sends Abigail away to live with her aunt.

Jack leaves the village to search for Abigail.
Jack cannot find her. He grows ill and dies.

Jack's ghost goes to Abigail and tells her
he has come to take her home.

When they get home, the ghost vanishes.
Abigail learns of Jack's death and dies of a broken heart.

The ghosts of Abigail and Jack haunt the churchyard.

Storyboards

Discuss how a storyboard can be used to develop a plot. Put an example of the start of a storyboard on the board and ask either pairs, groups or the whole class to work together to complete it. Either use an example of your own or use the example below, which is the start of a storyboard for a space adventure:

The crippled spacecraft makes an emergency landing on a planet.	It is surrounded by aliens.	The aliens board the spacecraft and imprison the crew.

Planning a story 2: the viewpoint

Explain how they have to decide who will tell the story and that stories can be told by one character from their point of view or by a narrator who can give several characters' points of view.

Put the following list on the board and discuss the two options open to them:

First-person narrator	**Third-person narrator**
One of the characters inside the story	An outsider who isn't in the story
Uses the pronouns I, me and we	Uses the pronouns he, she and they
Is only able to present their personal view of what happens	Can describe the thoughts, feelings and actions of all the characters.

Ask them to tell a partner whether they plan to use a first-person or third-person narrator.

Writing tip: be prepared to alter your plan

Explain that how you start a story will depend on what type of story it is. You may start by describing a person or a place. You may start with a conversation. It will depend on your plot.

Talk about the importance of not sticking too rigidly to your planned plot. Many novelists say that although they have a plot in their minds when they start to write they often alter it as they write. So be prepared to change your plot as you write, because a different idea comes to you.

Writing tip: drafting detailed sentences

Talk about how writers make their stories interesting by including plenty of description and choosing powerful and interesting words.

Write the sentence 'The man went into the room' on the board. Discuss how you could make this sentence more interesting by being more specific.

Ask who the man is. Is he a workman (e.g. a plumber)? Is he a robber? Is he a journalist? Is he a spy?

Ask how he is dressed. Is he smart or scruffy? Is there anything unusual about his clothes?

Ask how he is feeling and suggest adjectives you could use to describe his feelings. Is he sad? Frightened? Curious? Worried? Excited?

Discuss how the verb 'went' tells the reader nothing about how he went into the room. Ask them to suggest alternative verbs they could use which tell the reader how he entered the room, for example stumbled, charged, crept, marched.

Ask them to suggest adverbs to qualify the verbs, for example stumbled awkwardly, crept cautiously, marched briskly.

Point out that no details are given about the room. Ask what type of room it is. Is it a lounge, a kitchen, an office, a waiting room?

Ask if there is anything special about the room. Is it richly furnished, windowless, empty? Has it been ransacked?

Either draft an extended version of the sentence 'The man went into the room' and put it on the board, or use this sentence, which one class wrote, as an example: 'The injured prisoner limped painfully into the small windowless room.'

Setting the scene

Explain that at some point in a story, you will want to describe the setting where the story takes place.

Use **Activity sheet 30: setting the scene**. Talk about how you can set the scene for your story by describing the time and the place where the action takes place. Focus on the three descriptions in turn.

What impression of the moor is the writer trying to create? What details does she include in order to give that impression? Which words that she uses help to give that impression? What words would you use, besides bleak, to describe the moor (e.g. desolate, lonely, isolated, barren)?

What impression does the writer give of the fairground? Discuss the details that are included, and the words used, to give the reader an impression that the fairground is bustling and full of movement. Talk about how the author uses the senses in order to convey what the fair is like. Talk about the sights, sounds and smells that are described.

Discuss how the description of the town centre suggests that it is crowded and full of people.

Compare the three descriptions. Which do they think conveys the atmosphere of the scene most effectively?

Invite the pupils to write their own paragraphs in order to set the scene for a story. They could either choose their own scene or describe one of the following: an airport departure lounge, a building site, a forest, a shopping centre, a football stadium or a seaside scene.

Activity sheet 30: setting the scene

The moor

The mist swirled over the moor. You could scarcely see more than five yards ahead. The bare skeletons of trees appeared now and then at the side of the track. There was an eerie silence broken occasionally by the flapping wings of a bird that they disturbed from its roost. As night approached, it grew colder. What a bleak place, thought Jenny.

The fairground

The fair was in full swing. Young children chattered excitedly, teenagers laughed uproariously, and screams from the arms of the Torturer as it whizzed round mixed with the screeches from the dodgems as the cars thumped into each other. Lights flashed, music pounded, everywhere there was movement – the throwing of hoops, the bouncing of balls, the firing of rifles, the slithering down slides, the spinning roundabouts and the whirling big wheel. There were the smells too – of onions and burgers, of hot dogs and chips and the oily smell of the generators, as they whirred and hummed. Jamie put his hand in his pocket to feel the coins there. What should he go on first?

The town centre

The centre of the town was busy. At this time of year, during the school holidays, it was full of tourists. There was a group around the clock tower, waiting for it to strike the hour. Terry pushed his way passed them. There was a queue at McDonald's, which spilled out onto the street and a group had gathered to watch some street performers outside the entrance to the precinct. There was even a group of football fans who were making their way along the high street towards the stadium, singing and chanting as they went. He was already late. Would they still be there?

Describing characters

Talk about how as well as describing the setting in a story you will also want to describe the characters in it.

Discuss how you can develop a character in a story not only by describing their appearance, but by what they say and do during the story. Before you begin, however, you need to decide what sort of person the character is: Are they good or evil? Are they a hero or a heroine?

Ask the children to imagine they are writing a story about a boy or girl who wakes up one morning to find that they are in a different world. They meet someone. In pairs, ask them to build up a character.

Encourage them to talk about the character's personality. Put this list of different characteristics on the board and get them to choose the ones that fit their character:

good, honest, trustworthy, reliable, loyal, thoughtful, friendly;

bad, evil, wicked, dishonest, untrustworthy, unreliable, ruthless, cunning, sinister, unfriendly;

impulsive, reckless, well behaved, naughty, wise, foolish, timid, brave.

Then ask them to think about the person's appearance: Are they ordinary or odd? If so, what is strange about their appearance? Are they attractive or unattractive, handsome or ugly? What are they wearing? What two things are most noticeable about their appearance?

Use **Activity sheet 31: a character wheel**. Discuss the example of Scurvy Jim. Then invite the children in pairs to give the character they have created a name and to make a character wheel for that person.

When they have done so, ask them individually to write a paragraph in which they describe the character they have created.

Activity sheet 31: a character wheel

PERSONALITY

STRENGTHS/WEAKNESSES

MANNERISMS/VOICE

APPEARANCE

dishonest

wicked   nasty

cunning   villainous

loyal   aggressive   glares

brave   cruel

greedy   sly   scratches a lot

bad-tempered   deep growl

gets drunk   SCURVY   swears a lot
                      JIM

a determined fighter

straggly beard   sneers

dirty   tattered clothes

dishevelled   wrinkled

                    eye-patch

fierce

Describing the action

Writing tip: choose powerful verbs and adverbs

Put the following sentences on the board and invite the children to redraft them in order to make them more interesting by changing the verbs and adding adverbs (possible suggestions are included in brackets):

The rat ran across the kitchen. (scuttled, scampered, raced, scurried, dashed, darted, quickly, swiftly, rapidly, hurriedly)

The man went along the path. (strode purposefully, hurried anxiously, strolled thoughtfully, plodded doggedly, limped painfully, jogged steadily)

The waves hit the ship firmly. (battered furiously, smashed relentlessly, slapped incessantly, struck fiercely, hammered remorselessly)

The flood water came down the street. (poured, cascaded, flowed, swept, swirled, gushed, surged, rapidly, swiftly, mercilessly)

The pirate looked at the boy. (stared, glared, gazed, glowered, scrutinised, scowled, menacingly, maliciously, threateningly)

Writing dialogue

Discuss how the way a person speaks depends on their personality and background. Some people use standard English all the time, while others use a dialect all the time. Explain that, when you are writing a story, you can use the language a person uses when they speak as a way of indicating their character.

For example, say you are writing an adventure story in which two children are caught trespassing in the garden of a large house and are being questioned by someone:

'What the devil do you think you are doing? Can't you read? This is private property. I could have you arrested. Be off with you. If I find you here again, I shall be forced to report you.'

''ere, you two, what're you up to? This 'ere's private property. If they catches you, you'll cop it. Now, scram, before anyone sees you.'

Writing tip: punctuating speech

Explain that when you are writing a story, you often include what a person actually says or said. This is known as direct speech and you must use speech marks to show the words that they spoke. Discuss how speech marks are sometimes called *inverted commas*. For example: 'I cannot come out to play,' said Jane.

Explain the rules about how to punctuate direct speech by looking at an extract from a novel or using the example on **Activity sheet 32: punctuating direct speech**. It is an extract from a story called 'The Shed'.

Go through the rules for punctuating direct speech. Then ask the children to practise using speech marks by continuing the story by writing the conversation that the three children have as they discuss what they have found and what to do next.

Activity sheet 32: punctuating direct speech

1
Only put words that are actually
spoken inside speech marks.

2
Start a new
paragraph
when a new
person speaks.

'We can't go in there,' said Sam.

'Why not?' asked Abid.

'It's private property,' said Sam. 'Besides, the
door's locked.'

3
Use a small letter to start words
like 'said' and 'asked' after a
speech because they are in the
middle of a sentence.

Pat gave the door a push and it swung open.

'No, it isn't,' she said. 'Come on, I'm going to have
a look.' She switched on the torch and cautiously
stepped inside.

4
Begin each new speech with a
capital letter.

'What if someone sees us?' said Sam, nervously
looking back up the path.

Just then Pat turned round and whispered. 'Be
quiet. Just look at this!'

5
Always put the punctuation mark at the end of a
speech inside the speech marks.

Continue the story of the shed. Write the conversation the children have as they discuss what
they have found and what to do next.

Writing tip: use alternatives to 'said'

Talk about how 'said' is often overused when they are writing dialogue and how important it is to be aware of alternatives that you can use, most of which are more expressive.

Invite them to play 'Instead of said'. The aim of the game is to think of as many alternatives to 'said' as they can within a given time limit. The winner is the group which writes down the most. Use a dictionary if a word is disputed. Ten is average, 15 is good, 20 is very good and 25+ is excellent.

Suggested words include: announced, answered, babbled, bawled, bellowed, cried, declaimed, declared, exclaimed, gabbled, growled, grumbled, hollered, howled, interjected, interrupted, jabbered, mumbled, muttered, proclaimed, questioned, quipped, remarked, replied, roared, screamed, shouted, stuttered, wailed, whispered, yelled.

Writing challenges

1 Imagine you had a talking pair of shoes. Write a story about them without using the word 'the'.
2 You find what you think is a marble in your pocket. You hear a tapping from inside it and, as you examine it, a tiny creature begins to emerge. Describe it in 50 words.
3 Write a story in 99 words which begins 'Suddenly I saw ...'
4 Choose a word beginning with 'h', a word beginning with 'p' and a word beginning with 's'. Write a paragraph about a journey which includes the three words. Alternatively, open a dictionary and put your finger on a word at random. Do it three times and use the three random words in your story.
5 Ask a friend to choose a number between 50 and 100. Write a story about a mad scientist in that number of words.
6 Write a story about a flying cat, a rampaging robot or a pair of jumping jeans.

26 Play-scripts

A play-script is a written copy of the dialogue performed by the actors in a play.

Explain what a play-script is. Discuss how a play-script contains a list of the characters in the play and details of the setting where each scene takes place, in addition to the dialogue between the characters and any important moves that the actors make, for example when a person enters or exits.

Use **Activity sheet 33: the layout of a play-script** and talk about how to lay out a play-script. Point out the main features:

1   There is a list of the characters.
2   There are details of where the scene takes place.
3   The name of the person speaking is put in the left margin, followed by a colon.
4   Speech marks are not used.
5   You start a new line every time a new person speaks.
6   Details of any important actions that occur are put in italics or highlighted in some way.
7   Any instructions about how a person is speaking are put in brackets after their name.

Activity sheet 33: the layout of a play-script

The Broken Vase

The characters:

Jason, aged 11

Sophie, his sister, aged 12

Mrs Grayson, their mother

Scene: The living room of the Graysons' house.

Jason is bouncing a ball. Sophie is reading a book.

Sophie: Stop doing that. I'm trying to read.

Jason: Why? I'm not stopping you.

Sophie: It's annoying. That's why.

Jason: I'm bored.

Sophie: Well, go and do something then. Just stop bouncing that ball.

Jason: Why should I? Stop bossing me about.

Sophie (*exasperatedly*): Stop it, I said.

Jason (*picking up the ball and throwing it towards her*): Here. Catch.

Sophie drops her book, missing the ball, which knocks over a vase, smashing it.

Jason: Oh, no!

Sophie (*angrily*): Now look what you've done.

Jason: It's your fault. You should have caught it.

Sophie: Don't be stupid. You threw it.

Jason: What are we going to do? It's Mum's best vase.

Sophie: That's your problem. You'd better get the dustpan.

She picks up her book and starts reading again. Jason leaves the room, then comes back with a dustpan and brush. He bends down and starts picking up the pieces of vase.

Jason: Aren't you going to help?

Sophie: No.

Jason: What am I going to say? It's the one Gran gave her.

There is the sound of a door being opened and shut.

Jason: Oh no. Here she is.

Mrs Grayson (*calling*): Hello, I'm back.

(*Entering the sitting room.*) What have you two been up to while I've been out?

Writing tip: apostrophes

Talk about how when people speak, they often use contractions. For example, in the extract from *The Broken Vase* on Activity sheet 33 Sophie says 'I'm trying to read' instead of 'I am trying to read' and 'It's annoying' instead of 'It is annoying'. Explain that the rule is: when you use a contraction in your writing, you always put an apostrophe where a letter or letters are missed out. Ask the children to find other examples of the use of the apostrophe to indicate a contraction in the extract from *The Broken Vase*. Can they find 12?

Point out that the apostrophe in 'Mum's best vase' is an apostrophe showing possession, not an apostrophe indicating a contraction. (For further advice on the use of the apostrophe see Chapter 33.)

Use **Activity sheet 34: write your own play** to get the children to write their own play-scripts.

Activity sheet 34: write your own play

Choose your setting

Either choose your own setting or choose one from this list: school classroom, beach, market, forest, shopping precinct, fairground, old house, park.

Choose your scenario

What will be the main feature of your play? What will happen in it? Either choose your own scenario or choose one from this list: quarrel, accident, discovery, something gets lost, dare, something strange happens, quest, important event.

Choose your characters

Who your characters are going to be will depend on your chosen scenario. Here are some suggestions (but you need not stick to this list – you can add other characters too): teacher, a boy/two boys aged 11, a girl/two girls aged 11, a teenager/two teenagers, stallholder/shop owner, police officer/security guard/lifeguard/forest ranger, passer-by, old lady, homeless person, TV reporter, ambulance officer, person dressed as a clown.

Once you have decided on your setting, scenario and characters, you can start to draft your play.

Remember to lay it out as a script is laid out.

Curriculum opportunities

There are opportunities in many areas of the curriculum for improvising scenes that can then be developed as play-scripts. For example, the pupils can develop a scene in which two children who have seen a Viking warship land on a beach in north-east England tell the people in their village what they have seen and the villagers discuss what to do.

27 Poems

A poem describes an emotion, thought or idea through the pattern of words on a page, which is different from the way words are set out in a piece of prose.

Writing poems: experimenting with forms

Discuss how there are many different forms of poetry. Explain that there are two main types of poems – rhyming poems and non-rhyming poems.

Rhyming poems

Explain that rhyming poems are often divided into verses and that many poems have four-line verses. Use **Activity sheet 35: rhyming patterns** and discuss how four-line verses can have a number of different rhyme patterns.

Focus on pattern 1. Put another verse from the poem about 'The Dreaded Doubts' on the board, leaving out lines 2 and 4, as follows:

Will my teacher frown and say

_____? (I have to stay in and miss play?)

What if I fail the spelling test

_____? (Even though I tried my best?)

Ask the children to help you to complete the verse. Then see if the class can draft another verse to add to the poem. For example:

What will happen if I'm not able
To recite the seven times table?
What if I have a quarrel with Jill
Will she want to sit next to me still?

Note: The whole poem can be found in the Appendix at the end of the book.

Focus on pattern 2. Put the first two lines of some other verses from the poem about 'The Bamboozle' on the board and get the class to try to complete them:

The Bamboozle is a creature
Which is very hard to find ...

The Bamboozle is a creature
Which is very hard to see ...

The Bamboozle is a creature
Which does not make a sound ...

Note: The whole poem can be found in the Appendix at the end of the book.

Focus on pattern 3. After explaining the pattern, work with the whole class to complete this verse about a mad magician using the same rhyme pattern:

In his dark cave the mad magician dwells ...

Activity sheet 35: rhyming patterns

Many poems are written in four-line verses called quatrains. Four-line verses can have a number of different rhyme patterns.

Pattern 1

The first and second lines rhyme and the third and fourth lines rhyme.
    Example:

    At night-time, as I lie in bed,
    The Dreaded Doubts enter my head.
    What if we oversleep and then
    I shall be late for school again?

Pattern 2

The second and fourth lines rhyme, but the first and third lines do not rhyme.
    Example:

    The Bamboozle is a creature
    Which is very rarely seen,
    For it is very hard to tell
    Where a Bamboozle's been.

Pattern 3

The first and third lines rhyme and the second and fourth lines rhyme.
    Example:

    When the night is as cold as stone,
    When lightning severs the sky,
    When your blood is chilled to the bone,
    That's the hour when the witches fly.

Explain that there is a golden rule that you must follow when writing a rhyming poem: the rhyme must fit the meaning and sense of the poem.

Talk about what to do if you are stuck for a rhyme.

Make copies of **Activity sheet 36: writing up a rap**. Go through the poem and discuss the advice that John Foster gives on how to write a rap. Encourage the children in pairs or groups to write their own raps.

Writing challenges

Ask pupils to choose a well-known nursery rhyme and write a different version of it.

Explain what an epitaph is – an inscription or verse written on someone's gravestone. Invite them to write a rhyming epitaph for a dragon which can't breathe fire, a nursery rhyme character or a character from a fairy tale.

Activity sheet 36: writing up a rap

Snap it up! Clap it up! Rap it up, son!
And we'll wrap up a rap before the day is done.

Take a leaf from a book or a leaf from a tree,
A feather from a bird or a wave from the sea.
Take a dragon's fire or a witch's spell,
A lizard or a wizard or a wishing well.

You can take any subject that you choose.
But make up your mind, there's no time to lose.

Snap it up! Clap it up! Rap it up, son!
And we'll wrap up a rap before the day is done.

Don't hesitate. Let's make a start.
For rapping ain't so easy. Rapping is an art.
It's time for a rhyme. Don't sit on the fence.
But you've got to be sure that your rhymes make sense.

You've got to watch out. You've got to be wary.
If all else fails, there's a rhyming dictionary.
There are rhymes by the dozen, rhymes by the score,
Rhymes by the hundred, rhymes galore.

Snap it up! Clap it up! Rap it up, son!
And we'll wrap up a rap before the day is done.

Now you need some rhythm, you need a beat.
Get the drums drumming, start tapping your feet.
Let your hair down. Turn up the heat.
Skip along, trip along, dance down the street.

Now we're getting somewhere with our creation,
It's time for a little alliteration:

With a stomp and a stamp, a quiver and a quake,
A glimmer and a glitter, a shiver and a shake.
A grim grey gremlin's gruesome grin,
And a slithery snake shedding its skin.

Put it all together with a zip and a zap
With a flip and a flop, and a trip and a trap.
And we've rapped it up,
Rapped it up,
Wrapped up a rap.

Non-rhyming poems

Encourage the children to experiment writing non-rhyming poems such as cinquains, haiku, kennings and tanka.

Cinquains

A cinquain is a five-line poem containing 22 syllables in the pattern 2–4–6–8–2.

Use **Activity sheet 37: cinquains**. Ask the children what is the same about the poems on the sheet and help them to work out the pattern of a cinquain. Then discuss the poems with them. Which do they think is the most effective? Talk about the use of powerful verbs and adjectives and the use of similes in 'Stormy Night'. Discuss which cinquain has the most effective last line. Point out that there is more to cinquain writing than counting syllables and that a good cinquain expresses clearly a thought or a feeling. Then ask the children to draft their own cinquains.

Haiku

A haiku is a traditional Japanese form consisting of three lines which together add up to 17 syllables in the pattern 5–7–5. Put the two examples (below) on the board. Discuss the poems with the children. Which poem creates the better picture? Which poem do they prefer? Talk about the comparisons made in the poems. Which simile is the more appropriate? Discuss the verbs that the poet has chosen and the use of alliteration.

Challenge the children to write their own haiku. Stress that there is more to writing a good haiku than just counting the syllables and that an effective haiku is either descriptive, creating a picture, or powerful because of the thought or feeling that is expressed.

White butterflies sit,
Sipping from summer flowers,
Wings like yachts' sails.

Swallows dip and dive,
Swerve and swoop in summer skies,
Graceful as gymnasts.

Tanka

A tanka is a Japanese poetry form. Each tanka consists of five lines which together add up to 31 syllables, arranged in the pattern 5–7–5–7–7.

Study the tanka (below) with the class, then challenge them to write a tanka of their own, about either 'The Thunder Giant', 'The Fire Giant' or 'The Hurricane Giant'.

In his icy cave,
The Snow Giant stirs and wakes,
His freezing breath blows
Blizzards, obliterating
The world beneath a white shroud.

Activity sheet 37: cinquains

Study the four poems. Then try to write a cinquain of your own. Either choose your own topic or write a cinquain about an animal or bird, or about a feeling such as anger, greed, envy or hope.

'Stormy Night'
Gale force
Winds lash the bay.
Anchored boats strain their chains,
Like tether'd dogs unable to flee
Wind's whip.

'Dawn'
Dawn breaks.
Night shadows flee.
Birds chorus a welcome.
Day beckons weary travellers
With hope.

'Accident'
'It was
An accident,'
He cries, tears streaming down.
Sighing, his mother bends her head,
'I know.'

'Mountains'
Mountains
Tower skyward,
Their distant snow-capped peaks
Reminding us how very small
We are.

Curriculum opportunities

When studying the Anglo-Saxons talk about how they enjoyed listening to stories and poems about heroes such as Beowulf. Explain that one particular feature of Anglo-Saxon poetry was the use of kennings.

A kenning is a descriptive phrase or compound word used instead of a noun. Anglo-Saxon poets frequently used kennings, for example calling a river 'the swan-path', an arrow ' a battle-adder' and the sea 'the fish-realm'.

Put the poem 'Wind' on the board and discuss how a poem can consist of a series of kennings.

Then invite the children to write their own kennings poems. They can either choose their own topic, for example an animal, or one from this list: waterfall, snowstorm, flood, earthquake, fire.

'Wind'
Leaf-stealer
Flag-flapper
Hat-snatcher
Branch-snapper

Sea-stirrer
Wave-whipper
Surf-raising
Sail-ripper

Door-slammer
Window-batterer
House-shaker
Peace-shatterer.

28 Jokes

Invite the children to share some jokes they know and write some of them up on the board. Explain that all jokes have the same structure: they have a set-up, followed by a punch-line.

Discuss the structure of the jokes that you have put on the board or give some examples such as:

Where does the burger sleep? On a bed of lettuce.

What do you get when you cross a snake and a kangaroo? A skipping rope.

Explain that many jokes are based on a pun – the humorous use of a word to suggest another word that sounds the same or has the same spelling. Often, they take the form of a conundrum – a question which has a humorous answer based on a pun, such as:

Why do cows use door bells? Because their horns don't work.

When does it rain money? When there's a change in the weather.

Point out that the pun may be based on a phrase rather than a word, such as:

Why are dentists unhappy? Because they are always looking down in the mouth.

Use **Activity sheet 38: writing jokes**. Go through the example that is given on the sheet, then invite the children to draft their own jokes. They can write their jokes on the computer and put them together with other jokes they have found in a Book of Jokes, compiled and written by Class X.

Activity sheet 38: writing jokes

1 Pick a topic word; any one-word noun will do, e.g. ring.

2 Brainstorm potential punch-lines and puns that are associated with the topic you have chosen, e.g.:

engagement rings/wedding rings;

ring a bell;

telephone rings;

ring roads;

run rings round;

boxing rings;

ring tones.

Note: Don't worry at this stage about how the words and phrases you list might fit into your jokes.

3 Study this list of common joke types:

Knock, knock ...

What's the difference between ...?

Doctor, doctor ...

Waiter ...

Why did the ... cross the road?

Why is ... like ...?

Conundrums which begin Why ...? What ...? When ...?

4 Drafting the joke: Try to find a connection between one of the joke types and your list of punch-lines and other punch-lines that you may think of as you are writing. Choose the idea from your brainstormed list that seems to offer the most potential. In this case, you might choose 'the telephone rings'. Then, look at the various joke types and see if you can make a joke about hearing a telephone ringing or ringing someone up.

For example, is there a punch-line about visiting the doctor because you keep on hearing a telephone ringing? The doctor could offer to cure it by suggesting you answer the phone. So your joke would be: 'Doctor, doctor, I keep on hearing a telephone ringing.' 'Well, answer it then.'

That works quite well, but you could improve it, perhaps by mentioning the telephone in the answer rather than in the question. So your revised joke will be: 'Doctor, doctor, I keep hearing this ringing in my ears.' 'Well, answer the phone and it will stop.'

Alternatively, you may start thinking about trying to phone someone up and always getting the engaged tone. You make the connection with wearing a ring and being engaged. There's the possibility of a pun on the word 'engaged'. You look at the list of formats and select the 'Why is ... like ...?' format. You then draft the following joke: 'Why is a girl with a ring on her finger like a person you can't get through to when you ring them on the phone?' 'They are both engaged.'

Now, try to write some jokes of your own. Either choose your own one-word noun or use one of the following: ball, band, bank, bowl, chip, flea, foot, horse, light, match, pen, post, saw, stamp, tap, toe, well.

29 Traditional tales

Exploring the features of the different types of traditional story – fairy tales, myths, legends and fables – can provide a range of opportunities for creative writing.

Fairy tales

Discuss how fairy tales are traditional tales that include elements of magic or the supernatural, such as *Cinderella* and *Sleeping Beauty*.

There are a number of opportunities for various different kinds of writing during a focus on fairy tales.

After reading and discussing various fairy tales, you could present the pupils with a choice of writing activity by listing the following suggestions:

Write a letter from the Big Bad Wolf in which he apologises to Red Riding Hood for trying to eat her granny.

Write some diary entries that either Cinderella or one of the ugly sisters wrote about their experiences before, during and after the ball.

Write a letter to the police from the three bears demanding that they arrest Goldilocks for breaking into their cottage.

Write an e-mail from the handsome prince to his father explaining that he has found the castle he was looking for and is about to investigate it.

Write Jack's description of the giant and his castle.

Writing challenge

Encourage the children to use the internet to research fairy tales from other countries. Then challenge them to rewrite the fairy tale in 100 words or less.

Myths

Talk about how some stories are explanations of how natural features were created. These stories are myths and include stories about how the world was created, how night came and how animals got particular features, for example how elephant got his trunk.

Either read the children a myth from a book of myths or tell them the story of how the Wrekin was formed:

How the Wrekin was formed

The Wrekin is a hill in the county of Shropshire which is a well-known landmark. Long ago, there was no hill where the Wrekin is now. At that time giants stalked the land. People were careful not to offend the giants.

But a giant who was living in Shropshire heard a rumour that the people of the town of Shrewsbury were plotting to drive him away. He was so angry that he decided to get his revenge on them by damming the river Severn, so that it would cause a flood. He dug up a huge spadeful of earth and set off in what he thought was the direction of Shrewsbury.

The earth was heavy and he could not walk fast. He was getting fed up, when he met a passing cobbler. He asked the cobbler how far it was to Shrewsbury and whether he was going in the right direction. The cobbler did not trust the giant, so he told him he was going in the wrong direction and that, in any case, Shrewsbury was miles away.

When he heard this, the giant lost his temper and threw down the spadeful of earth where he was standing, before stamping off. And the spadeful of earth became the hill known as the Wrekin.

Talk about any myths that are told about landmarks in your area. The children can then research other myths on the internet, before either retelling a myth in their own words or writing their own myths.

They can either choose their own subject or write about one of the following:

How monkey got his tail

How darkness came

How tiger got his stripes

Why the sun is in the sky

Why birds sing

Why snake sheds his skin

Why ostrich buries his head

Legends

Explain that legends are stories about great heroes and heroines, kings and queens. Often, the legendary figure is based on a real person, such as King Arthur or Robin Hood. Discuss how different countries have different legendary figures. Introduce the Swiss legend of William Tell.

Use **Activity sheet 39: the legend of William Tell**. It contains two accounts of the legend which Janice and Abid wrote after researching it. Discuss the two accounts of the legend and why Abid's account of the legend is less interesting than Janice's. Talk about how Janice gives more detail whereas Abid sticks to the bare facts. Discuss how Janice has arranged her account in paragraphs and show them how Janice planned her account by making a flow chart:

Para 1: Introduction – who William Tell was

Para 2: How and why William was arrested

Para 3: The shooting of the apple

Para 4: Escape and leading the fight for independence.

Ask the class if they know any legends about national heroes, such as the legends about King Alfred and the burnt cakes, King Arthur and the Knights of the Round Table, Robert the Bruce and the spider, Finn McCool and the Giant's Causeway, and Robin Hood and his Merry Men. Encourage them to take it in turns to tell each other the stories that they know in as much detail as possible.

Invite them to choose a particular legend and to write their own version of it. They can research the legend to find out details that they can include in their versions. For example, Janice found the details about saluting the hat from a version of the legend of William Tell that she found on the internet. Encourage them to plan their versions by making a flow chart, as Janice did.

Ask them to invent a legend involving a quest undertaken either by a real historical character or an imaginary character called Brian the Bold. Use the following questions as prompts to help them to plan their legends:

1   What problem does the hero/heroine face?
2   What task(s) must the hero perform to solve the problem?
3   Where must the hero go in order to find the solution?
4   Who accompanies the hero on the quest?
5   Who or what do they encounter during their travels?
6   How do the people and/or the creatures they meet try to stop them achieving their goal?
7   How do they overcome the problems that they encounter?
8   What is their reward for successfully completing the quest?

The checklist can also be used when assessing the legends they have written.

Activity sheet 39: the legend of William Tell

William Tell was a crack shot with the crossbow. The Emperor of Austria wanted to make Switzerland part of his empire. William was a rebel who refused to recognise the Emperor as the ruler of Switzerland and was arrested. He was told he would be freed if he could put an apple on his son's head and split it. He shot and split the apple, but he was not set free. Later he escaped and successfully fought for Switzerland's independence.

(Abid)

Several hundred years ago, there was a man called William Tell who lived in Switzerland. He became a national hero, because he led the fight for Swiss independence.

The Emperor of Austria wanted Switzerland to be part of his empire. In each town in Switzerland, an Austrian hat was put on a pole in the town square. All the men in the town had to salute the hat to show that they accepted the Emperor as their ruler. William Tell refused to do so and was arrested.

The Austrian who arrested him had heard that William was the best crossbow marksman in the town. He agreed to let William go, if he was willing to put an apple on his son's head and shoot an arrow at it. William shot an arrow and split the apple, but the man broke his promise.

However, William managed to escape and led the Swiss to victory in their fight for independence.

(Janice)

Fables

Discuss how a fable is a story, most often with animals as characters, which has a moral or message in it, such as Aesop's Fables.

Tell them a well-known fable such as 'The Grasshopper and the Ant':

It was summer. Grasshopper was enjoying himself, hopping and skipping about in the sunshine, whistling a happy tune. An ant came along, puffing and panting as it carried an ear of corn to its nest.

'Come and play with me, Ant,' said Grasshopper. 'You don't want to waste your time working on a day like this.'

'Sorry,' said Ant. 'I'm busy storing up food for the winter. You should be doing the same.'

Ant went on his way and Grasshopper just laughed and went on playing.

When winter came, Ant had plenty of food, while Grasshopper didn't have enough.

Talk about the moral of this story. Ask the children to share any other fables that they know.

Encourage the children to write a fable. They will need to decide what the moral of the fable is going to be. They can either choose a moral themselves or can choose a moral from the list below:

Pride comes before a fall.

Look before you leap.

Better to be safe than to be sorry.

Don't put off till tomorrow what you can do today.

Beware of flattery.

Do not judge people by their looks.

Don't be envious.

30   Tongue-twisters

Explain what a tongue-twister is – a phrase, sentence or rhyme that is difficult to say because it contains words which have similar or repeated sounds. Discuss how tongue-twisters can be very difficult to say, especially if you try to say them fast. Ask them for examples of short tongue-twisters that they know and put them on the board, then add the following examples:

Red lorry, yellow lorry.

The cruel ghoul cooks gruel.

Flat flying fish fly faster than fat flying fleas.

She sells sea shells on the seashore.

Choose some of the tongue-twisters. Issue a time challenge. How many times can they say the particular tongue-twister correctly in ten seconds?

Discuss what makes these tongue-twisters difficult to say. For example, 'Red lorry, yellow lorry' is difficult to say, because it is hard to stop yourself making the mistake of saying 'lolly' instead of 'lorry'.

'The cruel ghoul cooks gruel' is difficult because of the repetition of the -ool rhyming sound. Discuss how you could make this even more difficult by adding some other -ool words. Make a list of -ool words, for example school, rule, pool, fool, cool, stool, drool, tool, Yule. Ask them to make suggestions as to how they could add words; for example: at Yule, the cruel school ghoul cooks cool gruel.

Remind them what alliteration is – the use of several words together that all begin with the same letter or sound. Discuss how the tongue-twisters 'Flat flying fish fly faster than fat flying fleas' and 'She sells sea shells on the seashore' are difficult because they contain alliteration.

Use **Activity sheet 40: tongue-twisters** to encourage the children to write their own tongue-twisters. Before asking individuals or pairs to write their own tongue-twisters, work with the whole class and draft examples of tongue-twisters on the board. Collect the tongue-twisters they write in a class book of tongue-twisters.

Activity sheet 40: tongue-twisters

Many tongue-twisters use alliteration – the use of several words that start with the same letter or sound. For example, these tongue-twisters use a single letter sound:

Singers sing several simple songs simply.

Down the deep dark damp dank den.

Make up your own tongue-twisters using words that start with the same letter.

Other tongue-twisters use the sounds produced by consonant blends – groups of two or three consonants that make a distinct consonant sound such as 'ch', 'fl', 'spl' or 'thr'. For example: 'Charlie chewed chewy cheese', 'Three thrushes' throats'.

Choosing one of the consonant blends from the list below, make lists of words that begin with that consonant blend and use some of them to draft your own tongue-twister:

bl br ch cl dr fl fr gl gr pl pr

sc sh sk sl sm sn sp st sw th tr tw wh wr

sch scr shr sph spl spr squ str thr

Other tongue-twisters include rhyming sounds which make them difficult to say. For example: 'Quick lick six sticks', 'Sue Shore was sure she saw a dinosaur'.

Choose a rhyming sound from the list below and work with a partner to draft a tongue-twister based on that rhyming sound:

-ack -air -ale -all -and -ate -aze

-eed -eek -eel -eer -ent -ess

-ick -ight -ill -ine -ing -ink

-oo -ool -oon -ore -own

-ude -ung -unk -use

Part Five

Writing correctly

31   Grammar

How the words of the English language work together in speech and writing is known as the structure of the language. The structure and the rules governing it are called its grammar. Knowledge of grammar can help children to write correctly. The activities in this section are designed to help children to understand some of the basic rules of English grammar and the terms used to describe them.

Sentences

Explain that there are four types of sentence, depending on what the purpose of the sentence is.

Write the four headings on the board, give an example of each type of sentence and ask the class to give you further examples. List them on the board:

Statement: I'm going to take the dog for a walk.

Question: Do you know where its lead is?

Command: Stop doing that.

Exclamation: Good dog!

Play 'Give me a sentence'. Divide the class into groups. Explain that you are going to give them a key word. They must write four sentences – a statement, a question, a command and an exclamation – each of which must contain the key word. For example, if the word is 'cake', they could write: 'I ate a chocolate cake. Where is the cake that was left over? Bake the cake in the oven for 15 minutes. What a delicious cake!'

Start with some common nouns, such as horse, car and moon, and then make the task more difficult by giving key words, such as different, absurd and hope.

Complex sentences

Explain that a sentence may be simple, compound or complex.

A simple sentence consists of one main clause. Example: 'The boy kicked the ball.'

Talk about how simple sentences follow the pattern of subject–verb–object. The boy (subject) kicked (verb) the ball (object).

A compound sentence consists of two or more clauses, joined by *and*, *but* or *so*. Each of the clauses is a main clause and the clauses are of equal weight. Example: 'The boy kicked the ball, but the ball hit the crossbar.'

A complex sentence consists of a main clause and one or more subordinate clauses. Example: 'Although the goalkeeper was beaten, the ball hit the bar, so the match ended in a draw.'

Point out that the main clause is 'the ball hit the bar' and that there are two subordinate clauses – one beginning 'although' and the other beginning 'so'.

A clause must normally contain a complete verb; for example 'I was playing football in the back garden' is a clause. But 'in the back garden' is not a clause. It is a phrase – a number of linked words that form part of a sentence.

Parts of speech

Words can be divided into word classes according to the way they are used in sentences. There are eight main word classes in English: nouns, verbs, adjectives, adverbs, prepositions, pronouns, conjunctions and articles. These are also known as the parts of speech.

Nouns

A noun is a naming word given to a person, place or thing. A noun can also be the name given to something abstract such as a feeling, such as sadness or hope, or a particular quality, such as honesty or loyalty.

Use the verse below to help you to explain the different types of noun that we use when we write.

> **'A noun'**
> A noun can name a common thing
> Like bird or boat or book or ring.
>
> A noun can be a person's proper name
> Like Amrita, Carl or Sue.
> It can also name a particular place
> Like Belfast or Waterloo.
>
> It can be a concrete physical thing
> Such as carpet, shirt or soap.
> Or it can be an abstract feeling
> Like ambition, love or hope.

Spot the nouns: put the following passage on the board and ask the pupils in pairs to list all the nouns or make copies of the sentences and ask them to circle all the nouns. Then discuss which nouns are common nouns, which are proper nouns, which are concrete nouns and which is an abstract noun. You can use different colours to highlight the different types of noun.

> A girl called Jennifer, who lived in a village called Scotby, rode her bicycle down a lane and over a bridge. She didn't see some sheep coming out of a field and she gave a cry of fear as she was thrown over the handlebars into a ditch.

Collective nouns: explain what a collective noun is – a word which describes a group of animals, people or things. Give some examples – a herd of cows, a gaggle of geese, an army of soldiers, a bunch of grapes. Ask the pupils to think of other examples and list them on the board, for example a swarm of bees, a flock of sheep, a team of footballers, a pack of cards.

Introduce them to some of the more unusual collective nouns that are used to describe groups of particular animals and birds, such as an intrusion of cockroaches, a parliament of owls, a bloat of hippopotamuses, a smack of jellyfish, a troop of kangaroos, a labour of moles.

Encourage the children to make up some collective nouns. For example, what would be appropriate names for groups of ghosts, elves, ogres, pirates, raptors, aliens, leprechauns, unicorns, gargoyles, dragons, trolls?

Verbs

Explain that a verb is a word which tells us what people or things are doing or have done.

Writing tip: avoid using got

Discuss how it is important in your writing to use verbs which accurately describe what a person is doing or has done. Explain that the word 'got' is a 'nothing' word. It tells you what the person did, but nothing else.

Put the passage below on the board and ask the children to suggest how it can be rewritten so as to make it more effective by each time replacing the word 'got' with a more descriptive word.

Jason got ready to go out. He got some money from his money box and got his coat. When he got outside, he got the bike from the shed. Then he got on the bike and set off to meet Trevor.

See the activity in Chapter 25 which encourages the children to use powerful verbs.

Writing tip: use the right tense

Talk about how verbs have different forms or tenses which tell you whether an action takes place in the present, the future or the past.

The tense you use will depend on what type of writing you are doing.

For example, autobiographical writing (see Chapter 3) and recounts (see Chapter 8) focus on events that have taken place in the past, so the past tense is used.

Non-chronological reports (see Chapter 23) are usually written in the present tense, with the exception of historical reports, which are written in the past tense.

Arguments (see Chapter 10) are presented mainly in the present tense, but you may use the past tense to describe an incident or give an example which supports your point of view.

Explanations (see Chapter 17) of what something does or how it works are written in the present tense.

Irregular past tenses

Some children make errors using the past tense of verbs which are irregular. Having been taught that the past tense is often formed by adding the suffix -ed, they apply this as a rule and produce errors such as 'bringed'. Or they think that because the past tense of ring is rung, then the past tense of bring should be 'brung'.

Use **Activity Sheet 41: past tenses crossword**. Explain that the answers consist of the correct past tenses of the verbs which are the clues.

Activity sheet 41: past tenses crossword

Clues across

1. fly
5. bring
6. ring
9. begin
10. throw
14. strike
15. eat
16. hit

Clues down

1. forget
2. tread
3. dig
4. think
7. give
8. win
9. break
11. rise
12. cut
13. sit

Writing tip: split infinitives

Explain that the infinitive of a verb is the form of the verb used after *to*. For example, to walk, to forget, to write.

If you put a word between the *to* and the verb, you are said to have split the infinitive, as in these examples: to boldly go, to anxiously wait.

Talk about how it was traditionally thought to be wrong to split infinitives. However, there is no grammatical reason for this so-called 'rule', so it is a matter of style.

Writing tip: active and passive

Discuss how verbs may be either active or passive.

In an active sentence, the person performing the action is the subject of the verb. Example: 'Susan dropped the vase.'

In a passive sentence, it is the person or thing that is acted upon which is the subject of the verb. Example: 'The vase was dropped by Susan.'

Active sentences are much more common when you write than passive sentences, for two reasons. First, passive sentences often sound more awkward and less natural than active sentences. For example, 'Amir picked the ball off the floor' sounds more natural than 'The ball was picked off the floor by Amir'. Second, your writing can become dull if you overuse the passive.

However, the passive voice can be useful when you are writing about something which happened in the past, such as: 'Many children were evacuated during the Blitz.'

It can be useful, too, when you want to emphasise something at the start of a sentence, such as if you are quoting an example to support your viewpoint in an argument: 'Thousands of accidents are caused by young drivers every year.'

Adjectives

An adjective is a word that describes or gives information about a noun.

Explain that by choosing powerful adjectives when you are writing, you can make your descriptions of people and places more interesting and effective. See, for example, the activity on choosing adjectives to use when trying to make a holiday destination sound attractive in an advertisement (Chapter 9).

Encourage the children in groups to list alternatives to these commonly used adjectives: wonderful, big, awful, cold, weak, small, strange, dull. Compare their lists in a class discussion.

Making comparisons

Explain how we use adjectives to make comparisons. For example, we say: 'John caught a large fish', 'Jim caught a larger fish', 'Jeremy caught the largest fish'.

When we are comparing two things, we often add -er to the adjective. This is called the comparative: small + -er = smaller, loud + -er = louder.

When we are comparing more than two things, we often add -est to the adjective. This is called the superlative: small + -est = smallest, loud + -est = loudest.

Not all adjectives have a comparative and a superlative form. When we make comparisons with these adjectives that do not have a comparative and a superlative form, we use more and most: 'Jeremy's fish was more difficult to catch than Jim's', 'Jeremy's was the most difficult fish to catch'.

Similarly, we can write: 'Jeremy's fish was more heavy than Jim's fish', 'Jeremy's fish was the most heavy fish that was caught that day'.

But it is wrong to write: 'Jim's fish was more heavier than John's fish', 'Jeremy's fish was the most heaviest that was caught that day'.

The rule is: When you make a comparison you only need to use one comparative.

✓ He made a bigger mistake.

✗ He made a more bigger mistake.

Similarly, when you use a superlative you only need to use one superlative:

✓ She is the cleverest in our class.

✗ She is the most cleverest in our class.

Put these sentences on the board and ask the pupils individually to decide which are correct and which are wrong:

1 This pencil is sharper than that one.
2 Andrea runs more faster than Chloe.
3 Gina is the most tallest of the girls.
4 It was the longest night of the year.
5 Janita took the shortest time to complete the test.
6 It was the more harder task.
7 It was the most stupidest thing I've ever seen.
8 It was easier than I expected.

Adverbs

An adverb is any word which adds to the meaning of a verb, adjective or other adverb by telling *how*, *why*, *when* or *where* an action takes place.

Explain that there are four main types of adverbs:

1 adverbs of manner, which explain how something is done, e.g. carelessly, confidently, nervously;
2 adverbs of time, which explain when something is done, e.g. yesterday, late, already;
3 adverbs of frequency, which explain how often something is done, e.g. sometimes, often, occasionally;
4 adverbs of place, which explain where something is done, e.g. there, outside, downstairs.

Make a large chart to go on the wall. Draw four columns on it labelled 'Adverbs of manner', 'Adverbs of time', 'Adverbs of frequency' and 'Adverbs of place'. Encourage the children to list in the appropriate column any adverbs that they encounter in their reading.

Discuss how using adverbs can make your writing more interesting. See the activity on adding powerful verbs and adverbs when describing the actions in a narrative (Chapter 25).

Writing tip: word order matters

Explain that it is important to be careful about where you put adverbs or you can cause confusion.

Put this sentence on the board: 'His hair needs cutting badly.' Discuss why the sentence is confusing. Explain that the adverb 'badly' refers to 'needs' rather than 'cutting' so it should have been written 'His hair badly needs cutting'.

Here are five more confusing sentences. Put them on the board and talk about where the adverb should be put in order to avoid confusion.

Please go slowly round the bend.

Simon sleeps loudly on the bed and snores.

He ran into the building quickly.

She sat and waited for the door to open anxiously.

Tom left the new trainers on the bus he bought yesterday.

Prepositions

A preposition is a word used before a noun or pronoun to make a phrase to do with either a place (at home), a time (before lunch), a position (inside the bag) or a way of doing something (by train).

Explain what a preposition is, then give the class **Activity sheet 42: prepositions** to complete.

There are 17 prepositions in the poem: from, down, up, round, through, behind, on, along, across, over, under, before, after, in, beside, at.

Writing tip: prepositions at the end of sentences

Some people think that it is wrong to end a sentence with a preposition. However, ending a sentence with a preposition rarely makes it harder to understand its meaning. In fact, it can sound more awkward and less natural. For example, 'That's the school I go to' sounds more natural than 'That's the school to which I go'. Similarly, 'What are you looking at?' sounds more natural than 'At what are you looking?' So it is suggested that a better rule to follow is to place the preposition where it sounds more natural.

Activity sheet 42: prepositions

Circle the prepositions in this poem.

'Prepositions'

I have a mission to find a preposition.

Is it hiding from me

Down the lane or up a tree?

Round the corner, through the door,

Behind the sofa, on the floor?

Along the road, across the street,

Over my head, under my feet?

Before lunch or after tea,

In the news or on TV?

Beside the sea, at the fair,

Prepositions are everywhere!

Pronouns

Explain that a pronoun is a type of word that is used in a sentence in place of a noun or noun phrase.

Talk about how there are three types of pronoun – personal pronouns, which refer to a person or persons (I, you, he, she, we, they), possessive pronouns, which show possession (my, mine, yours, his, hers, ours, theirs) and relative pronouns, which show the relation between people and objects (who, which, whose). Ask the pupils to draw three columns labelled personal pronouns, possessive pronouns and relative pronouns. Then read the following passage slowly and ask the children to identify the pronouns and put them in the appropriate columns.

> She peered at the footprints which were clearly visible and wondered whose they were. Her instinct told her that she should follow them. But it is not my decision whether we should go on, Gemma thought. She turned to Jim, who was behind her. 'What do you think?' she asked. 'It's our last chance,' he said.

Explain that pronouns are useful when we write, because they make it possible for us to avoid repeating nouns or noun phrases that would make our writing awkward and long-winded.

Give an example. Put the following passage on the board and talk about how pronouns can make it shorter and less awkward:

> Jason was climbing a tree in Jason's garden. Jason fell out of the tree and Jason's leg was cut. Jason's mother saw Jason fall and Jason's mother phoned for an ambulance.

Writing tip: I and me

Explain that I and me are often used incorrectly. The rule is: I is always used as the subject in a sentence and me as the object in a sentence.

✓ Jane and I went to the cinema.

✗ Jane and me went to the cinema.

✓ My parents took Jane and me to the circus.

✗ My parents took Jane and I to the circus.

Put these sentences on the board and ask the class to complete them using either I or me:

> ___ put my lunch-box into my bag.
>
> My dad asked ___ if I had any homework.
>
> My friend and ___ are going to play football in the park.
>
> I have to do my chores before Mum gives ___ my pocket money.
>
> James is allowed to go there, so why can't Sam and ___?

Standard English

Begin by explaining that whatever form of writing you are asked to do, you must always use correct standard English grammar. Standard English is the particular variety of English that is used in almost all publications and in the broadcasting media. Other varieties of English, such as the dialects used in certain parts of the country such as Merseyside have their own grammar, which differs from standard English. You may use expressions which are acceptable when speaking your own dialect, but which are not acceptable in your writing.

Common errors

Use **Activity sheet 43: common errors** to point out some common grammatical errors and **Activity sheet 44: spot the error** to test pupils' understanding of these common errors.

More common errors: singular or plural?

1 **Each and every**
   Put these sentences on the board:

   Each of the boys were late for school.

   Each of the boys was late for school.

   Every monkey likes bananas.

   Every monkey like bananas.

   Discuss which of the sentences are correct and explain that *each* and *every* are singular and are always followed by a singular verb.
   The rule is that the following words are all singular and are followed by a singular verb: each, everybody, one, every, anyone, someone, everyone, anybody, somebody.

2 **None**
   Explain that some people believe that since *none* is a contraction of *not one* it is singular and should always be followed by a singular verb. However, *none* is also used to mean *not any*, so it is possible to write either 'None of the class has done their homework' or 'None of the class have done their homework'.

Activity sheet 43: common errors

1 **Off, Of and Off of:**
Off means 'away from' as in 'get your feet off the table'.
Of is used to show possession, as in 'the owner of the dog'.
But there is no such expression as 'off of' in standard English.
✓ 'Keep off the grass' is correct.
✗ 'Keep off of the grass' is not correct.

2 **Should've/Should of**
When we say *should've* instead of *should have*, it sounds as though we are saying *should of*. So sometimes people write *should of* when they should have written *should've*. Similarly, it is a mistake to write *would of* or *could of* instead of *would've* and *could've*.

3 **Those/Them**
In standard English it is not correct to say or write 'them people'; you must write 'those people'.

4 **Was/Were**
In some dialects, people say 'we was', 'you was' or 'they was'. In standard English, you must say or write 'we were', 'you were' or 'they were'.

5 **Did/Done**
In some dialects, people say 'I done', 'you done' and 'we done'. In standard English, you must write 'I did', 'you did' and 'we did'.

6 **Double negatives**
In some dialects, people use a double negative when they want to emphasise that they have not done something. For example, they say 'I haven't done nothing'. In standard English, the two negatives cancel each other out, so you must say or write 'I haven't done anything'.

7 **Ain't**
In standard English, it is not correct to use the expression 'ain't'. Instead you should say or write 'hasn't' or 'haven't', 'am not', 'isn't' or 'aren't'.

8 **Past tense**
In standard English, when speaking or writing about the past, you must use verbs with their proper past tense form or past tense ending. For example, instead of writing 'He come round to ask if I'm going out', you must write 'He came round ...'

9 **Subject/Verb agreement**
In standard English, if the subject is singular the verb form must be singular; if the subject is plural the verb form must be plural. For example, it is incorrect to write 'She have a brother and a sister' or 'We has a dog'. Instead, you must write 'She has a brother and a sister' or 'We have a dog'.

10 **Wrote/Writ**
In standard English, 'writ' is not the past tense of the verb to write. The past tense is either 'wrote' or 'written'.

Activity sheet 44: spot the error

Each of these sentences contains an error. The error is underlined. Write the correction at the end of each line.

1   I <u>ain't</u> done my homework yet.

2   Pass me one of <u>them</u> biscuits, please.

3   Trevor and <u>me</u> went round to see Jason.

4   I <u>writ</u> a note that Mr Wilson wanted to see me at break.

5   I told him that I wasn't there and that I never did <u>nothing.</u>

6   He <u>give</u> me extra homework, because I wasn't paying attention.

7   I <u>should of</u> gone to netball practice but I forgot.

8   It bounced <u>off of</u> his racket and into the net.

9   My older brother <u>have</u> a motorbike.

10 He <u>done</u> very well in the test and was third.

11 We <u>was</u> sure that the film started at 4 o'clock.

12 I <u>come</u> in late, so I missed assembly.

Modifiers

A modifier is a word or phrase that is added to provide more information about the word or phrase to which it refers. For example, an adjective such as 'small' modifies a noun such as 'boy'. Similarly a phrase may provide further information about a person or thing. For example, in the sentence 'Descending from the spacecraft, the astronaut walked toward the group of aliens', the modifier adds the information that the astronaut was descending from the spacecraft.

Misplaced modifiers: A misplaced modifier is a word or words that are badly placed in a sentence so that they could refer to more than one thing, so the meaning is unclear.

Put the following sentences on the board, discuss why they are ambiguous, then ask the children to suggest how to rewrite them and punctuate them, so as to make the meaning clear:

The boy told the dog to sit licking an ice-cream.

Failing to jump the fence the jockey was thrown by the horse.

Weeping uncontrollably the teacher told the boy never to cheat again.

Visitors to the museum can learn about the dinosaurs listening to a recorded commentary.

The man thought he saw a ghost in the garden cleaning the windows.

The girl stroked the cat reading a magazine.

The boy boarded a bus going to see the dentist.

Only children with adults are allowed to go on this ride.

32 Spelling

Spelling rules

Discuss why English spelling is difficult because so many words are not spelt as they sound. The reason for this is the way that the English language has developed, borrowing words from many other languages. For example, two words which come from other languages and that are difficult to spell are *yacht*, which comes from Dutch, and *meringue*, which was originally French.

Explain that there are a number of rules which can be helpful with spelling, but there are almost always some exceptions to the rule.

Use **Activity sheet 45: spelling rules** to introduce some spelling rules that are useful.

Activity sheet 46: useful spelling tips offers a number of tips that can be useful when learning to spell difficult words.

Activity sheet 45: spelling rules

The 'i' before 'e' rule

You put 'i' before 'e' except after 'c'. Examples: believe, chief, field, piece, shield; ceiling, deceive, receipt. Exceptions: seize, weir, weird.

Adding a prefix

A prefix is a group of letters which are added to the front of a word and which change its meaning. For example, the prefix *sub* means 'under' so *submarine* means under the sea.

When you add a prefix to a word, you do not change the spelling of the word. Examples: dis + solve = dissolve, mis + shape = misshape.

However, when you add the prefixes 'all' or 'well', they only have one 'l'. Examples: all + ready = already, well + come = welcome.

Goodbye final 'e'

A suffix is a group of letters which are added to the end of a word, which change its form or its meaning.

To a word which ends with an 'e', when you add -ing say goodbye to the final 'e'. Examples: move + -ing = moving, take + -ing = taking. Exceptions: If a word ends in -ee, -oe or -ye, you don't drop the 'e' when you add -ing, so see + -ing = seeing, canoe + -ing = canoeing and dye + -ing = dyeing.

Dropping the final 'l'

When you add the suffix -full to the end of a word you drop the final 'l'. Examples: restful, joyful, hopeful.

Changing 'y' to an 'i'

When you add a suffix to a word which ends in a consonant followed by a 'y', you change the 'y' to an 'i'. Examples: cherry + es = cherries, hurry + ed = hurried, beauty + ful = beautiful, fury + ous = furious, happy + ness = happiness.

But this rule does not apply when you add the suffix –ing. Example: hurry + ing = hurrying.

Activity sheet 46: useful spelling tips

1 Divide words up into syllables. For example, *re-mem-ber*, *e-vac-u-ate*, *sud-den-ly*, *re-com-mend*, *in-de-pen-dent*.

   Watch out for words with disappearing sounds. For example, there are certain words in which vowel sounds are ignored, such as *bound* **a** *ry*, *conf* **e** *rence*, *int* **e** *rest*, *av* **e** *rage*. In some words, a consonant sound is ignored, e.g. *gover* **n** *ment*, *i* **s** *land* and *reco* **g** *nise*. You can help yourself learn to spell these words by pronouncing them in an exaggerated way, stressing the sound which is usually ignored.

2 Learn spelling pictures to help you to remember difficult words. For example, *necessary* is spelt with one **c**ollar and two **s**leeves.

   Find words within words that will help you to remember how difficult words are spelt. For example, *sol**die**rs* die, a *p**ie**ce* of pie, there is a rat in sepa**rat**e, a **secret**ary can keep a secret, the CIA have spe**cia**l agents, a mate you are = a mate u r = amateur, **to get her** = together, **ass ass I nation** = assassination.

3 Deliberately mispronounce a word, so as to remember how it is spelt. Examples: Wednesday *WedNESday*, *garAGE*, lang U AGE. This can be helpful when words have a silent letter in them. Examples: knob *ker-nob*, gnome *gee-nome*, science *sky-ence (sci-ence)*, biscuit *bis-coo-it*, fascinate *fas-cee-in-ate*, friend *fri-end*.

4 Use sentences or phrases to help you to spell difficult words. For example:

   arithmetic **a** **r**at **i**n the **h**ouse **m**ay **e**at **t**he **i**ce **c**ream

   beautiful **b**ig **e**ars **a**nd **u**gly **t**eeth **I** **f**ind **u**tterly **l**ovely

   because **b**ig **e**lephants **c**an **a**lways **u**nderstand **s**mall **e**lephants

   chaos **c**yclones **h**urricanes **a**nd **o**ther **s**torms **c**reate chaos

   ocean **o**nly **c**at's **e**yes **a**re **n**arrow

   rhythm **r**hythm **h**elps **y**our **t**wo **h**ips **m**ove

   For individuals, who are struggling with particular words, you can make up phrases. For example, a pupil struggling with the word 'field' was helped by her teacher making up the phrase '**f**rogs **i**n **e**very **l**ittle **d**itch'.

5 Use words within words, or other memory tricks, to help you to spell homophones. For example:

   De**ss**erts (e.g. puddings) have two spoonfuls of sugar whereas de**s**erts (e.g. the Sahara) only have sand.

   Here is a place, but you h**ear** with your **ear**.

   A princi**pal** at school is a **pal**, but a princi**ple** you believe or follow is a ru**le**.

   A p**A**rked c**A**r is stationary, but Env**E**lop**E**s are station**e**ry.

   There is a place. Think of **here** being in t**here**. But **their** shows possession and a **heir** is in th**eir**.

6 Use jingles or rhymes to help you to remember how to spell difficult words:

difficulty Mrs **D**, Mrs **I**, Mrs **FFI**,

Mrs **C**, Mrs **U**, Mrs **LTY**

disappear Mrs **D**, Mrs **I**, Mrs **S**, Mrs **A**,

Mrs **PP** and Mrs **EAR**

7 Remembering the number of times that letters occur in certain words can help you to spell them. For example, emba**rrass** has two *r*s and two **ss** – two rosy reds and two simply scarlets; **scissors** has one cutting **c** and four sharp **ss**; **success** has three **ss** (super superb scholars) and two **cs** (clever clogs).

8 Use these rhymes to help you to remember words which have silent letters in them:

In han**d**kerchief, san**d**wich and We**d**nesday,
We don't pronounce the **d**.
In lam**b** and lim**b**, and dum**b** and num**b**,
We don't pronounce the **b**.

We don't pronounce the **k**
in **k**nife, in **k**nock and **k**nee.
In whis**t**le and cas**t**le and of**t**en,
We don't pronounce the **t**.

We don't pronounce the **n**
in autum**n** and in hym**n**.
We don't pronounce the **h**
in w**h**irr and w**h**isk and w**h**im.

We don't pronounce the **h**
in **h**onest and **h**our too
and in **w**rist, **w**rap and **w**rite
we don't pronounce the **w**.

Homonyms

A homonym is one of a group of words with the same spelling but a different meaning. For example, the word 'play' can be a noun meaning a performance that is put on in a theatre or it can be a verb meaning to take part in, as in 'I play tennis'.

Explain that a lot of jokes are based on homonyms. Ask if anyone knows the answers to these questions:

1   Why is a river lazy?
2   Why are vampires mad?
3   What sort of fruit would you find in a diary?
4   Why did the owner give his dog a pair of gloves?
5   Where do fish wash?
6   What is the strongest bird?
7   Why did the musician keep his trumpet in the fridge?
8   What do liars do when they die?
9   Why do idiots eat biscuits?
10 Why did the corn get cross with the farmer?

(Answers: 1 It never leaves its bed. 2 Because they are bats. 3 Dates. 4 It was a boxer. 5 In river basins. 6 A crane. 7 Because he liked cool music. 8 They lie still. 9 Because they are crackers. 10 Because he kept pulling its ears.)

Encourage them to make up pairs of sentences to show the two different meanings of these homonyms: present, match, fair, pupils, bank, left, right, flat, bear, rose, trip, watch, seal.

Homophones

Explain that homophones are words which sound the same but are spelt differently and usually have different meanings. Give some examples: rain, rein, reign; maid, made; to, two, too.

Put the passage (below) on the board and discuss which words are spelt wrongly, because the writer has used the wrong homophone. Use a coloured pen to highlight the words and discuss what the correct spellings should be.

> The tied was going out. The son was shining and I sore a yacht sale buy. Their were sum people on the beech but only a phew. There wood be more later.

Because the words in the passage are homophones, a computer spellchecker would not pick them out. Challenge the children to try to confuse a spellchecker. Ask them to write a similar passage in which there are a number of wrong homophones and to put it onto a computer to see whether the computer spots their deliberate mistakes.

Here is the start of such a passage: 'He did not no wear he was ...'

Give out copies of **Activity sheet 47: homophone puzzles** for the class to complete.

Use **Activity sheet 48: common confusions** which presents an activity on the spelling of pairs of words that often cause confusion.

Activity sheet 47: homophone puzzles

These puzzles are based on homophones. Write the answers in the space provided. The first one has been done for you.

A tree that is beside a stretch of sand at the seaside. **beech/beach**

The victim of a predator kneeling down to worship.

An infringement in a football match committed by a bird.

Two identical socks lying beside a fruit.

A TV programme in several parts advertising a breakfast food.

A flower that is planted in straight lines.

How to move a broken-down car with part of your foot.

A story about the bushy part of a squirrel.

A screech of agony made by a large sea creature.

A bucket with a very white face.

A young person and a person who works underground.

Activity sheet 48: common confusions

Some words are commonly confused because they sound or look similar. Can you fit them into the sentences correctly?

accept/except: Everyone was able to go on the trip _____ Tariq. I was unable to _____ the invitation, as I was on holiday.

alter/altar: There were flowers on the _____ in the church. We had to _____ the appointment, because I had football practice.

bath/bathe: If you have a shower rather than a _____ you use less water. It was too rough for us to _____ in the sea.

brake/break: The front _____ on his bicycle was broken. Be careful not to drop it or it will _____.

lose/loose: If we _____ the match, we will be disappointed. I have a front tooth which is _____ and will come out soon.

meter/metre: We parked our car at a parking _____. The winner threw the javelin at least a _____ further than anyone else.

of/off: The notice said we must keep _____ the grass. He is one _____ our best players.

plane/plain: The rain in Spain falls mainly on the _____. She wore a _____ white dress. The _____ landed at the airport.

pray/prey: The fox crept towards its _____. The vicar said, 'Let us _____'.

quite/quiet: It was very _____ in the hall as we waited for assembly to begin. I am _____ good at drawing, but not as good as Thelma.

33　Punctuation

Explain that we use symbols in our writing known as punctuation marks in order to make it possible for people to understand and make sense of what we have written.

Discuss why punctuating your writing is important.

Put this passage on the board without the punctuation in it.

> we were playing football when the rain started before we reached the shelter we were soaked so we went in there was nothing we could do so we waited until it stopped suddenly the sun came out but we decided not to play again the pitch was too muddy

Discuss why it is difficult to read. Ask them in pairs to punctuate it by deciding where to put a capital letter at the start of each of the sentences and a full stop at the end of each one. Then compare their punctuation of the passage in a group discussion.

Put a copy of these two rhymes on the classroom wall to remind them of how to use capital letters and full stops.

Capital letters
The capital letters were causing a fuss,
saying, 'You must remember how to use us
at the start of a name like Imran or Paul,
or the name of a place such as Crewe or Porthcawl.
You must use us when you start new sentences too.
Don't forget to use us whatever you do.'

Full stops
At the end of each sentence, the full stops all shout,
'Please use one of us. Do not leave us out.
You must not be under any delusion.
If you do not use us, you will cause great confusion.'

Commas

Explain how the comma is used in a number of ways. It is used to break up lists of words and phrases and to separate the clauses in a complex sentence to make the sentence easier to read.

- Commas are used to separate the words in a list.
- The list may be a list of nouns, e.g. 'On our way to Glasgow, we passed through Crewe, Preston, Penrith and Carlisle','He packed his shirt, shorts, socks and boots in his sports

bag'. Note: In lists like these you don't need a comma after the 'and' joining the last two items.

- It may be a list of adjectives, e.g. 'The woman had thick, curly, brown hair'.
- It may be a list of adverbs, e.g. 'Slowly, thoughtfully and carefully he read the letter again'.
- Commas are used to separate a list of phrases in a sentence: 'We spent the day swimming in the sea, digging a sandcastle, searching for shells and playing crazy golf', 'He ran down the street, across the bridge, down some steps, through the gate and into the park'.
- Commas are used to mark off a short phrase which is used in the middle of a sentence to add some extra information: 'The players, even the best ones, found it hard to control the ball', 'Josephine, a talented dancer, reached the finals'.
- Commas are used in complex sentences before the conjunctions which link the clauses together: 'While he was waiting at the bus stop he saw his friend, so he waved to her, but she didn't wave back.'

Commas after connectives: Explain that you often need to put a comma after a connective that is used at the beginning of a sentence.

Put a comma after these connectives when you use them at the start of a sentence:

Time connectives: firstly, secondly, meanwhile, finally, lastly.

Contrasting connectives: however, nevertheless, on the other hand, alternatively.

Expanding connectives: moreover, furthermore, in addition, additionally, for example, for instance, likewise, similarly.

Causal connectives: consequently, thus, therefore, for that reason, as a result.

Concluding connectives: to sum up, in conclusion, in short, in summary, to conclude.

A common error with commas: You cannot put a comma between two sentences. You must use a full stop.

✗ Teresa went out into the corridor, she knew that Emilia would be waiting for her

✓ Teresa went out into the corridor. She knew that Emilia would be waiting for her.

Use **Activity sheet 49: commas** to test the children's understanding of how to use commas.

Activity sheet 49: commas

Put commas in these sentences to punctuate them correctly:

1 For breakfast I had a glass of orange juice a bowl of cereal a slice of toast and a banana.
2 We went swimming in the pool to the cafe for a meal looked round the shops then caught a bus home.
3 Although we were already late there was nothing we could do about it except wait for the next bus.
4 However in this instance I am prepared to make an exception.
5 John who was next in line waited anxiously not knowing what to expect.
6 Cautiously Selena slid back the bolt paused and taking a deep breath pushed open the door.
7 The men dug frantically using picks shovels spades and their bare hands.
8 The strange man had big bushy eyebrows a long lean face with a scar and held a large sharp knife.
9 Hanif was sure someone was inside but when he rang the doorbell there was no answer so he took out his mobile phone punched in the number he had been given and left a message.
10 In conclusion I think animals such as elephants lions and tigers should not be kept in captivity unless the species is threatened with extinction.

Discuss how to use semi-colons, colons, brackets and dashes. Then give out copies of **Activity sheet 50: punctuation practice** for the children to complete.

Semi-colons

Explain that a semi-colon is used to mark a pause that is longer than a comma, but is not as long as a full stop.

It has two main uses. One of its main uses is to separate items in a list where each item is described by a phrase rather than a single word. For example: 'During the trip you will have the opportunity to explore the area; to visit the castle ruins; to take a boat trip round the lake; and to visit the souvenir shop.'

The other use of the semi-colon is in sentences which have two main clauses which are of equal importance and are not linked by a conjunction. For example: 'Some people think the film was better than the book; others preferred the book', 'Earlier I had a bad headache; now it has gone'.

Colons

A colon is used to introduce a list of items or examples: 'You will need to bring: a pencil and paper, a camera, waterproof clothing, a packed lunch and a swimming costume', 'Examples include: guineas, sovereigns, crowns, half-crowns, shillings and sixpences'.

A colon is used to extend a sentence by explaining or expanding what has been previously mentioned: 'There are two ways of looking at it: either he was offside or he wasn't', 'I agree with you entirely, he should have asked your permission: whatever reason he had for being absent'.

Brackets

Discuss how brackets are used to enclose extra information that would otherwise interrupt the flow of a sentence. Give them the following examples: 'Roald Dahl (1916–1990) wrote many children's books, including *Charlie and the Chocolate Factory*', 'The top must be screwed into place (see figure 2), before the legs are fitted', 'See the description (page 17) for further details'.

Talk about how the information, which is included in brackets, can be removed from a sentence without altering its meaning.

Explain that another use of brackets is to indicate alternatives and to give abbreviations and give the following examples: 'The player(s) must accept the umpire's decision at all times', 'The Royal Society for the Prevention of Cruelty to Animals (RSPCA) deals with thousands of cases of cruelty every year'.

Dashes

Explain that a dash is used to interrupt the continuity of a sentence and that it is more often used in informal rather than formal writing: 'We've won – you'll never guess – a trip to Disneyland!', 'I'm going to stay with my Aunt Betty – you met her last year – on her farm'.

Activity sheet 50: punctuation practice

Correct these sentences by punctuating them properly:

1   queen victoria 1837–1901 reigned for longer than any other british monarch
2   in victorian times some children were forced to work as chimney sweeps others had to work in factories and mines
3   next fix the screws to the leg see diagram
4   i went to the shop the one on the corner but they hadn't any left either
5   at school she was a gifted tennis player she was good at netball too
6   you must answer all the questions in the time allowed thirty minutes
7   anyone who fails to return the slip by the deadline next tuesday will not be able to go on the trip
8   the competition will be over by six thirty seven at the latest
9   he had three choices either to accept the ticket he was offered to go to another performance or not to go at all
10 there are a number of ways of crossing the english channel you can fly you can go by ferry you can go by train through the tunnel or you can swim

Apostrophes

Apostrophes of omission

Put this rhyme on the board:

> Leaving a letter out of a word is permitted,
> If you put an apostrophe where it's omitted.

Explain that when you join two words together and leave a letter or letters out, you replace it/them with an apostrophe.

Ask them to tell you examples of common contractions and make a list of them on a large sheet of paper which you can display on the classroom wall.

Common contractions include:

aren't, can't, couldn't, didn't, doesn't, don't, hadn't, hasn't, isn't, shan't, shouldn't, weren't, won't, wouldn't

I'm, you're, he's, she's, it's, we're, they're

I'll, you'll, he'll, she'll, we'll, they'll

I've, you've, he's, she's, it's, we've, they've

I'd, you'd, he'd, she'd, it'd, we'd, they'd.

Play Jumping Jacks. Choose somebody to be hot-seated as Jumping Jack. Make up some sentences with the class in which the apostrophe of omission occurs and ask individuals to come and write them on the board. As they write, Jumping Jack has to jump up and tell them when they should put in an apostrophe.

For example: 'It's cold in here, isn't it? We'll have to put our coats on, won't we? We shouldn't have opened the window. I'll close it. That's better. We're warmer now.'

Apostrophes of possession

Explain that apostrophes are also used to show possession. When we want to tell a reader that someone (or something) belongs to someone (or something) we use an apostrophe, either followed by an 's' or on its own. Put the examples (below) on the board, together with the poem, and explain that the basic rules are: 1) when a noun is singular you add 's; 2) when a word is plural and ends with an 's', you add only an apostrophe.

Write some examples on the board: Jack's grandfather, Sam's ruler, the bird's nest, the bicycle's wheel, the pupils' desks, the teachers' cars, the spiders' webs, the trees' branches.

Put this rhyme on the board for them to learn:

> If a noun is singular, you do not have to guess,
> You always have to add apostrophe s.
> But when a noun is plural and ends with an s, you see,
> You only add an apostrophe.

Explain that there is a third rule: 3) when a noun is plural and ends with a letter other than an 's' you add 's.

Put some examples on the board: the men's hats, the children's laughter, the sheep's wool, the crowd's roar.

To test pupils' understanding of the use of the apostrophe to show possession, read out the following sentences and get the pupils individually to write the sentences, then put the answers on the board.

His bicycle's chain came off.

The shed's door was open.

The boy's tooth was aching.

His father's face was angry.

Sam's hands were dirty.

The Christmas tree's lights had fused.

The children's books are on the shelves.

Sally's mum has lost her keys.

Grandpa's glasses were on the table.

The twins' clothes were in their room.

Apostrophes and plurals

When you add 's' to a word to form its plural you do not need to add an apostrophe as well.

A greengrocer who advertises apple's, pear's and orange's for sale has misused the apostrophe. He should have written apples, pears and oranges.

The shoe shop that offers shoes', slippers' and boots' for sale is also misusing the apostrophe. It should have written shoes, slippers and boots.

'The punctuation blues'

Make copies of **Activity sheet 51: 'The punctuation blues'**. The poem can be used to remind pupils of the different punctuation marks and when to use them. Invite groups to prepare performances of the poem. Encourage them to be inventive, for example, by making placards and by dividing up the poem so that some parts are spoken in unison and other parts are spoken by pairs.

Activity sheet 51: 'The punctuation blues'

'The punctuation blues'
I got up this morning, but I should have stayed in bed,
For punctuation marks were whizzing round my head.
I woke up this morning – I was so confused
I think I had a dose of the punctuation blues.

There were apostrophes here. There were apostrophes there.
Apostrophes were scattered everywhere.
Some were attempting to give me a lesson
On how they can be used to show possession.
While another group were milling about
Saying use us when a letter's left out.

The capital letters were causing a fuss,
Shouting, 'You must remember how to use us
At the start of names like Imran and Paul,
And the names of places like Hadrian's Wall.
And don't forget us, whatever you do
You must use us to start your sentences too.'

There were groups of commas in front of a list
Saying we mustn't be left out, omitted or missed.
We'll show you in sentences where there are pauses
By indicating breaks between phrases and clauses.

A pair of exclamation marks were dancing about
And in a loud voice I heard one shout,
'Stop! Come here! Do as I say!
Don't do that! Get out of my way!'

There were question marks everywhere too,
Asking: Where? What? When? Why? Who?
There were semi-colons looking for clauses
Between which they could show longer pauses.
There were hyphens playing hide-and-seek
And speech marks waiting for people to speak.

I got up this morning, but I should have stayed in bed,
For punctuation marks were whizzing round my head.
I woke up this morning – I was so confused
I think I had a dose of the punctuation blues.

© 2014, *Let's Write*, John Foster, Routledge

Proofreading

Use **Activity sheet 52: proofreading** to give pupils practice at spotting grammatical errors and punctuation and spelling mistakes.

Activity sheet 52: proofreading

Read the following passage, looking for grammatical errors, punctuation and spelling mistakes. When you find a mistake, write the correct word and the correct punctuation in the space provided. The first correction has been done for you.

It were a race against time if he failed to deliver the message they wood walk strait

It was

into a trap he new every thing depended on him so he hurried on

down the parth his knee was aching from wear he had hurt it when he fell its no good he

thought im not going to make it suddenly a light apeared in the distance who would be

coming down the trak at this time of nite he wondered

the car screeched too a halt two men in uniform jumped out brandishing guns

quick get In one of them shouted theres no time to lose

It was only when he was in the car that he relised his mistake

Confusing sentences

Give out copies of **Activity sheet 53: confusing sentences**, which contains ten examples of confusing sentences with explanations as to why they are confusing. Ask the pupils to rewrite them.

Explain that in examples 1–4, commas can be used to make the meaning clear. In examples 5–7, the meaning is not clear because there are dangling participles. In examples 8 and 9, the meaning is not clear because of the way that pronouns are used. In example 10, the sign is not punctuated properly.

Here are possible ways of rewriting the sentences, so that they are not confusing:

1 *Either* Waiting for a bus, I saw a man in the street *or* I saw a man in the street who was waiting for a bus.
2 I know a man, named Smith, with a dog.
3 I want to buy string and wrapping paper, for his present.
4 We sat at a cafe watching the ships, drinking lemonade and reading.
5 We were sitting in the grandstand and the pitch seemed far away.
6 As I was walking down the street, there was a cat that I could see.
7 He was standing on the platform. The train was late.
8 *Either* When he met the teacher in the corridor, he was late *or* When he met the teacher in the corridor, the teacher was late.
9 She gave her message to her mum, which told her mum where her mum had to go.
10 The sign said 'Slow. Children crossing.'

Activity sheet 53: confusing sentences

1   I saw a man in the street waiting for a bus. *Who is waiting for the bus? The person speaking or the man in the street?*

2   I know a man with a dog named Smith. *Who is called Smith – the man or the dog?*

3   I want to buy string and wrapping paper for his present. *What does the person want the wrapping paper for – as a present or to wrap a present?*

4   We sat at a cafe watching the ships drinking lemonade and reading. *Are the ships drinking lemonade and reading?*

5   Sitting in the grandstand the pitch seemed a long way away. *Is the pitch sitting in the grandstand?*

6   Walking down the street there was a cat that I could see. *Who is walking down the street – the cat?*

7   Standing on the platform, the train was late. *Who is standing on the platform? Is it the train?*

8   When he met the teacher in the corridor he was late. *Who is late? The teacher or the person who met the teacher?*

9   She gave her message to her mum which told her where she was to go. *Who is being told where to go? The daughter or the mum?*

10 The sign said 'Slow children crossing'. *Are the children slow or does the sign ask drivers to slow down?*

Either reword or punctuate the sentences so that they are not confusing and make their meaning clear.

34   Vocabulary building

Encourage the children to keep vocabulary books in which they write new words which they encounter both in class and in their private reading.

Word walls

Word walls are a useful tool not only for extending pupils' vocabulary, but also for reminding them of how words are spelt. Word walls can be used to collect words connected with a particular topic, for example a history topic, such as the Egyptians, or a more general topic, such as water, to collect powerful words, such as adjectives to use in a particular type of writing, for example descriptions, or, more generally, to collect new words that will help to extend pupils' vocabularies.

Whichever type of word wall you decide to use, encourage the children to add new words to the wall when they encounter them. Once you have sufficient words on the wall, there are a number of games you can play to help them to remember the words and what they mean.

What's the word?

This is a game for the whole class. Explain that you are going to choose a word from the word wall. You will give them a number of clues; they then have to write down what the word is.

For example, if the topic is water, you might choose the word *evaporate*. You explain that the word is on the word wall, then give them clues, such as:

The word is a verb.

It has four syllables.

It has nine letters.

It rhymes with accelerate.

It describes how a liquid changes.

You then choose another word from the wall and so on. You could make the game into a competition between groups, awarding a point for each correct answer by individuals. The group with the most points is the winner.

Hot seat

This is an alternative version of 'What's the word?' Choose one of the class to sit in the 'hot seat' with her back to the 'word wall'. One of the other members of the class chooses a word from the word wall and goes up to the wall and points to it. The aim of the game is for the person in the hot seat to identify the word by asking the others questions, such as 'Is it a noun?', 'How many syllables has it?', 'Does it begin with the letter a/b/c etc.?', 'Does it mean the same as ...?' or 'Does it rhyme with ...?'

They might go on to ask more specific questions, such as 'Is it a piece of clothing?', 'Is it an animal?' or 'Is it a building?' until they identify the word. Keep a count of the number of questions the person in the hot seat has to ask before they identify it. Then, invite some other members of the class to sit in the hot seat. The person who asks the fewest questions before identifying the word is the winner.

Find the word

This is a dictionary game. Give the pupils dictionaries. Choose a word from the word wall, then give the children clues. They have to identify the word and find it in the dictionary. For example, say you chose the word *detest.* You might give them clues such as:

> This word means to hate or dislike.
>
> A synonym of this word is loathe.
>
> It has six letters.
>
> It begins with d.
>
> It rhymes with arrest.

Synonyms and antonyms

Explain that a synonym is a word which means the same or nearly the same as another word, for example small/tiny/minute/little or grotesque/horrible/hideous/deformed.

An antonym is the opposite of a synonym. It is a word which means the opposite of a synonym.

Ask the children to complete **Activity sheet 54: rhyming synonyms and rhyming antonyms** to help them to understand what synonyms and antonyms are.

Answers: Synonyms: curious/furious; gigantic/frantic; wild/mild; wary/scary; cheeky/sneaky.

Antonyms: bold/old; neat/sweet; straight/late; fast/vast; brave/grave; rude/shrewd.

Talk about how you can find synonyms in a thesaurus – a reference book in which words are grouped according to their meanings. Put this sentence on the board and discuss how a thesaurus can help you when you are writing:

> A thesaurus is apt, liable, inclined to repeat, regurgitate words that are synonymous, but it can be useful, helpful to refer to when you are writing and cannot discover, find, locate the most appropriate, suitable word.

Point out how a thesaurus can help you to find more powerful words. Put this sentence on the board: 'He took hold of my arm.' Ask one of the class to look up 'hold' in a thesaurus and to read out the words which are synonyms of hold, for example grip, grasp, clutch, seize, grab, clasp. Ask the class to choose one of these words as an alternative to use in the sentence.

Explain what a cliché is – a tired word or phrase that has been used so often that it has lost most of its meaning – and that a thesaurus can also be useful in helping them to avoid using clichés. Make copies of **Activity sheet 55: tired words** for the pupils to complete.

Activity sheet 54: rhyming synonyms and rhyming antonyms

Can you find synonyms to fill the gaps in this poem? The poem is written in pairs of lines which rhyme, known as rhyming couplets. So the words you find to end the lines of each couplet must rhyme, as *glad* and *sad* do in the first two lines.

I am pleased. I am glad.
I am miserable. I am sad.

I am inquisitive. I am _____.
I am angry. I am _____.

I am colossal. I am _____.
I am frenzied. I am _____.

I am savage. I am _____.
I am meek. I am _____.

I am watchful. I am _____.
I am fearsome. I am _____.

I am impudent. I am _____.
I am sly. I am _____.

Can you find antonyms to fill the gaps in this poem?

I am timid. I am _____. I am young. I am _____.
I am untidy. I am _____. I am bitter. I am _____.
I am crooked. I am _____. I am early. I am _____.
I am slow. I am _____. I am tiny. I am _____.
I am cowardly. I am _____. I am frivolous. I am _____.
I am polite. I am _____. I am stupid. I am _____.

© 2014, *Let's Write*, John Foster, Routledge

Activity sheet 55: tired words

Suggest other words that you could use in your writing instead of the tired, overused words listed in the left-hand column. Use a thesaurus to help you to find alternative words. The first one has been done for you.

Tired words	*Other words you could use*
amazing	astonishing remarkable extraordinary
awesome	
bad	
beautiful	
big	
cool	
good	
great	
lovely	
nice	
super	
weird	

Ambitious ants

Play the sentence game 'Ambitious ants'. The object of the game is to make up sentences of five words beginning with the same letter of the alphabet. The sentences must consist of an adjective, a noun, a verb, an adjective and a noun. For example, 'Ambitious ants ate angry apricots'.

Choose a letter and ask groups to see how many sentences they can make up within a set time limit, for example 10 or 15 minutes. Encourage them to use dictionaries to find words that they could use. You can then play another round of the game by choosing another letter. The winner is the group which makes up the most sentences.

Pass the prefix

This is a game in which the children practise building new words by adding prefixes to existing words. The players sit in a circle. One of the players has to choose a prefix, such as anti-, and to say a word, which begins with that prefix – such as anti-freeze. They then pass the prefix to the person on their left who has to say another word that begins with anti. They then pass the prefix to the person on their left, who has to supply another word beginning with anti-. The round continues until a person cannot think of a word beginning with anti-. That person then drops out, a new prefix is chosen and the game continues until there is only one person left who is the winner.

Words of the week

Use a section of the word wall for words of the week. Ask each of the children to choose a word of the week. Encourage them to use a dictionary to help choose their words and to look up the meanings of other people's words. You can hold a competition in which the children have to write sentences in which all the words are used correctly, and at the end of the week announce who is the Word Champion of the Week.

Word lists

Invite the children either individually or in groups to make lists of words, for example ten frightening words. Other words that they could make lists of are polite words, bumptious words, violent words, grumpy words, glamorous words, heavy words, soft words or harsh words. When they have made their lists they can then compare them, before putting them on the word wall.

Word exchange

When the children have completed their first drafts of a creative piece of writing, such as a story or poem, you can invite them to take part in a word exchange. This involves bartering words which will make their writing more interesting. They can barter as many words as they like. This activity works best with more able pupils.

Letter poems

Encourage the children to extend their vocabularies by writing poems about various letters of the alphabet.

Use **Activity sheet 56: 'If I were an A'**. Explain that the poems are from a series about the letters of the alphabet. Talk about how 'If I were an A' lists a number of adjectives beginning with A. You can then invite the children to write a similar poem about another letter. Either they can choose a letter or use one of the following to start their poem: 'If I were a B, I'd be boisterous and bossy ...', 'If I were a C, I'd be cunning and cantankerous ...'. Encourage them to look in the dictionary to find adjectives to include in their poems.

Focus on 'I am a J'. Talk about how it differs from 'If I were an A'. Point out that as well as adjectives beginning with J, it also includes nouns and verbs that start with J. The children could work in pairs to produce similar poems about another letter.

Focus on 'If I were an S'. Discuss how the poet uses alliteration throughout the poem. Suggest that the children try to write another poem about a letter, such as T or R, in which they use a lot of alliteration. Alternatively, work with the class to draft a similar poem on the board. Again, encourage them to use dictionaries to find words that could be included.

Activity sheet 56: 'If I were an A'

Study these poems which are about letters of the alphabet. Use them as models to write your own poems about letters of the alphabet.

'If I were an A'
If I were an A
I'd be angry and annoying
I'd be arrogant and abrasive
I'd be aggravating and abhorrent
I'd be acrimonious and abusive
I'd be abysmal and abrupt
I'd be abominable and atrocious
I'd be appalling and argumentative
I'd be absolutely awful
Thank goodness I'm not an A.

'I am a J'
I am J.
I am a joker.
I am jovial and jocular.
I jink and I jiggle.
I juggle and I joggle.
I jitter and I jigger.
I jingle and I jangle.
I'm a jaunty jewel.
I'm a jolly jester.
I am J.

'If I were an S'
If I were an S I would be
A sleek seal surfing in a steel grey sea
A seagull strutting on a sandy shore
A scarecrow stretching in the summer sun
A shiver of soft snow
A swooping swallow
A silent statue
The shadow of a sail.

© 2014, *Let's Write*, John Foster, Routledge

35   Setting targets

Self-assessment plays an important part in the development of children's writing skills. If pupils are involved in assessing their work, they will be able to understand their strengths and weaknesses, and what they should focus on working to improve. Individuals can then be set writing targets.

You can use **Activity sheet 57: my writing skills** as a checklist for pupils to use and then discuss with you before setting them writing targets.

Activity sheet 57: my writing skills

Use this checklist to identify which writing skills you have developed and which you need to work on to improve your writing.

- I understand that we write for different purposes, such as to inform, to persuade, to explain or to tell a story.
- I understand that we write in different ways for different audiences.
- I understand that there are different stages in the writing process and I draft, redraft and proofread my writing.
- I know the difference between informal and formal writing.
- I can punctuate sentences properly, using capital letters, full stops, commas, question marks and exclamation marks correctly.
- I know how to divide my writing into paragraphs.
- I can use a range of different connectives.
- I use a varied form of openings.
- I use a wide vocabulary when I write.
- I include powerful adjectives and adverbs in my writing.
- I avoid using clichés.
- I know how to use apostrophes correctly.
- I avoid using slang and text-speak in my writing.
- I understand the difference between a simile and a metaphor and use similes and metaphors when I write.

What are your strengths and weaknesses as a writer?

Identify two things you could do to improve your writing.

Appendix

'The Dreaded Doubts'
At night-time, as I lie in bed,
The Dreaded Doubts enter my head.
What if we oversleep and then
I shall be late for school again?

Will my teacher frown and say
I have to stay in and miss play?
What if I fail the spelling test,
Even though I tried my best?

What will happen if I'm not able
To recite the seven times table?
What if I have a quarrel with Jill?
Will she want to sit next to me still?

What if I come out at quarter past three
And no one is there waiting for me?
At night, as I'm trying to get to sleep,
Into my mind the Dreaded Doubts creep.

'The Bamboozle'

The Bamboozle is a creature
Which is very rarely seen,
For it is very hard to tell
Where a Bamboozle's been.

The Bamboozle is a creature
Which is very hard to find.
It ambles slowly through the woods
And leaves no track behind.

The Bamboozle is a creature
Which is very hard to see,
For its skin is brown and wrinkled
Like the bark upon a tree.

The Bamboozle is a creature
Which can change its colour too.
In fields it turns as green as grass
And disappears from view.

The Bamboozle is a creature
Which does not make a sound,
As it carefully puts each padded foot
Down upon the ground.

The Bamboozle is a creature
Which does not leave a scent,
So you can't tell when the path forks
Which is the way it went.

The Bamboozle is a creature
Which is very rarely seen,
For it is very hard to tell
Where a Bamboozle's been.

Index

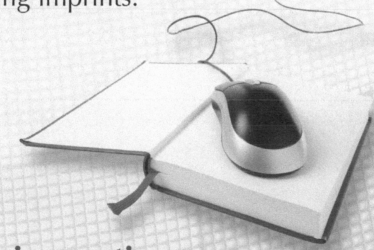